GREAT BOOK OF
MAZES

Roger Moreau

Sterling Publishing Co., Inc.
New York

10   9   8   7   6   5   4   3   2

Published by Sterling Publishing Company, Inc.
387 Park Avenue South, New York, N.Y. 10016
Material in this collection was adapted from
Mountain Mazes © 1996 by Roger Moreau
Save the Earth Mazes © 1996 by Roger Moreau
Great Explorer Mazes © 1997 by Roger Moreau
Jungle Mazes © 1997 by Roger Moreau
Space Mazes © 1997 by Roger Moreau
This edition © 1997 by Sterling Publishing

Sterling ISBN 0-8069-6117-1

CONTENTS

4

SPACE MAZES

Roger Moreau

Sterling Publishing Co., Inc.
New York

Contents

INTRODUCTION

Mankind has set foot on and explored Earth's moon on several occasions, but no planet beyond it. Yet much has been learned about our solar system thanks to unmanned space probes that have landed on some of the planets and flown by others. Also, the Hubble space telescope has helped to broaden our knowledge of deep space. But for every question that has been answered, many new ones have arisen. If we are to learn more, someone must be found with the courage and determination to be the first to explore the rest of our solar system and beyond.

That someone is you!

Get ready to go on the most exciting adventures imaginable. Be prepared to leave this planet Earth via the space shuffle and dock at an orbiting space station. There you will board a single-seat star cruiser capable of speeds beyond that of light. Your itinerary will take you on a tour of our solar system and into the vast reaches of the universe.

So that you can successfully plan your trip, it is important for you to learn some basic facts about our solar system and deep space. This information can be found on page 10. Once you have studied these facts, carefully follow your flight plans and the rules regarding each destination you visit.

May you have a great trip and safe return!

THE SOLAR SYSTEM

The solar system is made up of a medium-size star we call the Sun, nine known planets and their moons, and asteroids and comets. The planets, their moons, and the asteroids and comets revolve around the Sun and are held in place by its gravitational pull.

The nine planets that revolve around the sun are classified as either inner or outer planets. The four inner planets—those closer to the sun—are Mercury, Venus, Earth, and Mars. Separating the inner and outer planets is a belt of asteroids. Asteroids are simply rocks that range in size from hundreds of miles in diameter to less than one. Beyond the asteroids are the remaining five outer planets—Jupiter, Saturn, Uranus, Neptune, and Pluto.

Of the nine known planets, only the inner planets have solid surfaces that a spacecraft could land on. Of those, Mercury has furnace-like temperatures because it is so near the sun. Venus, with an eternal cloud cover that causes a greenhouse effect, also has a sizzling surface temperature. Mars appears to be the most likely planet where human exploration might be possible. Most of the other planets are whirling balls of gas.

Fortunately, you will be equipped with a special suit that enables you to explore Mercury, Venus, Earth's moon, Mars, and the asteroids. To explore the other planets, you'll have to stay in your spacecraft.

THE SOLAR SYSTEM
Comparative size and order from the Sun

Sun
Size: 1,400,000 km
865,000 miles

	Distance	Size
Mercury	57,900,000 km	4878 km
	36,000,000 miles	3032 miles
Venus	108,200,000 km	12,100 km
	67,000,000 miles	7,520 miles
Earth	149,600,000 km	12,756 km
	93,000,000 miles	7,928 miles
Mars	227,900,000 km	6,787 km
	141,500,000 miles	4,218 miles
Asteroids		
Jupiter	778,300,000 km	142,800 km
	483,700,000 miles	88,751 miles
Saturn	1,427,000,000 km	120,600 km
	886,900,000 miles	74,953 miles
Uranus	2,870,000,000 km	51,800 km
	1,783,000,000 miles	32,194 miles
Neptune	4,504,000,000 km	48,600 km
	2,799,000,000 miles	30,205 miles
Pluto	5,900,000,000 km	3,000 km (?)
	3,668,000,000 miles	1,865 miles (?)

Flight Plan Map

Find the path to each solar-system feature in order, from the Sun to Pluto. You can go underneath and over the top of each feature where indicated.

Space Shuttle

Board the space shuttle by following the correct fuel line to the ladders. Climb the ladders to enter the shuttle. You cannot go through any black partitions.

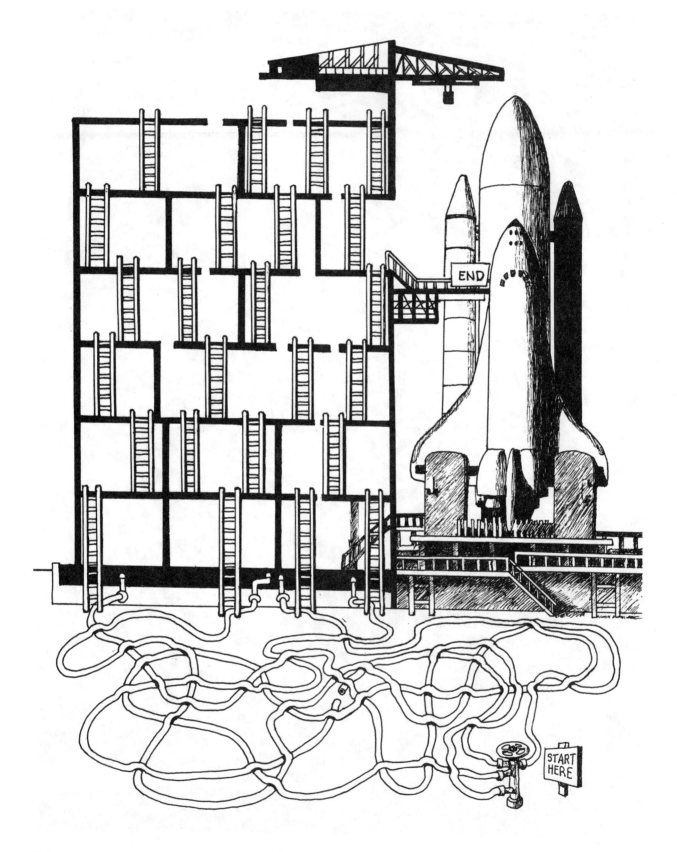

Space Station

Find a clear path to the distant space station, avoiding contact with any satellites.

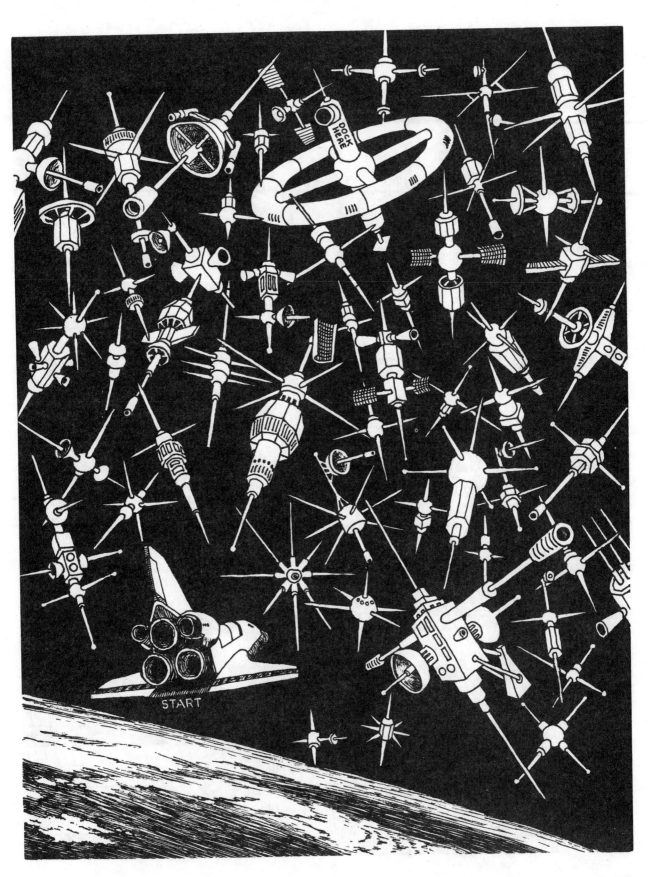

Departure

This space station has not been completed, but the countdown has begun. You have 10

seconds to board the star cruiser. Find the right path to the cruiser. You can cross from one path to another by walking across the single planks. Hurry!

Tour of the Sun

Tour the Sun without burning up. To do this, stay on the white paths.

Tour of Mercury

Tour the planet Mercury. Once you leave the space cruiser, find a clear path around its

surface. Then return to the space cruiser. This place is pretty hot during the day, so you'd better hurry.

Tour of Venus

Molten lava is bubbling up all over the surface of Venus. Avoid the lava and explore the planet until you can find your way back to the space cruiser.

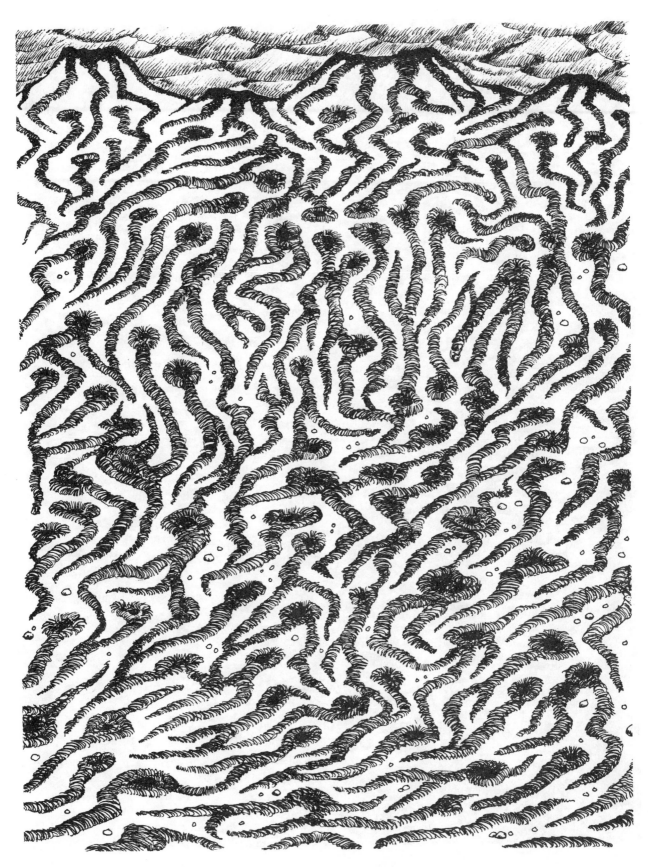

Tour of Earth's Moon

The surface of Earth's moon is filled with craters. Find your way between the craters and return to the space cruiser.

Tour of Mars

The largest known volcano in our solar system is Olympus Mons on Mars. Find a clear path to the top of the volcano and back to the space cruiser.

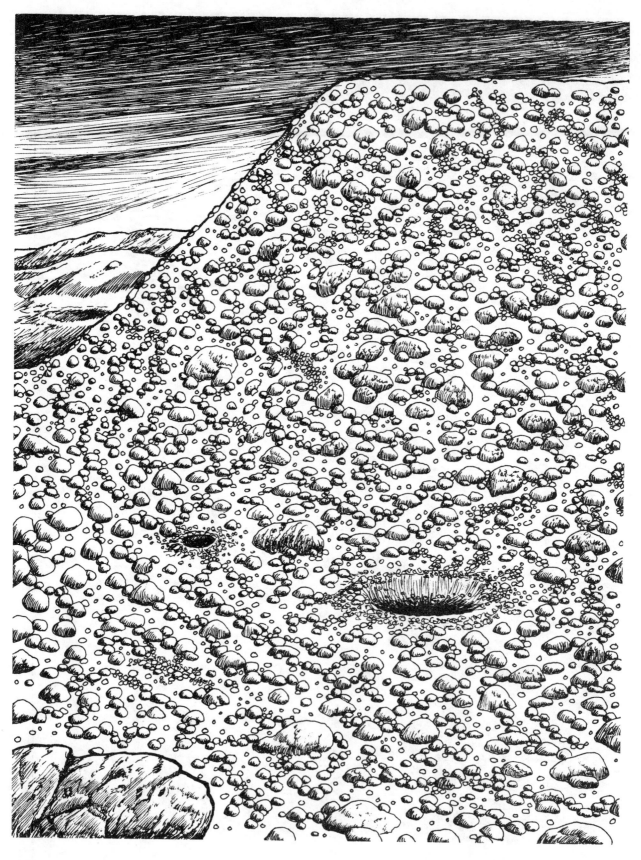

START   END

Asteroids

Find your way from asteroid to asteroid and back to the ship. Travel only on the asteroids that appear to be touching each other.

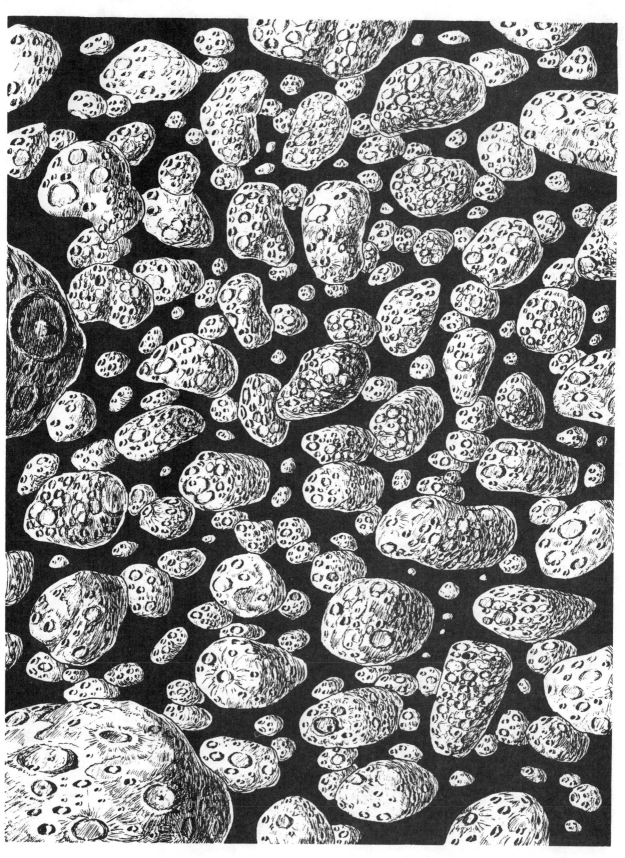

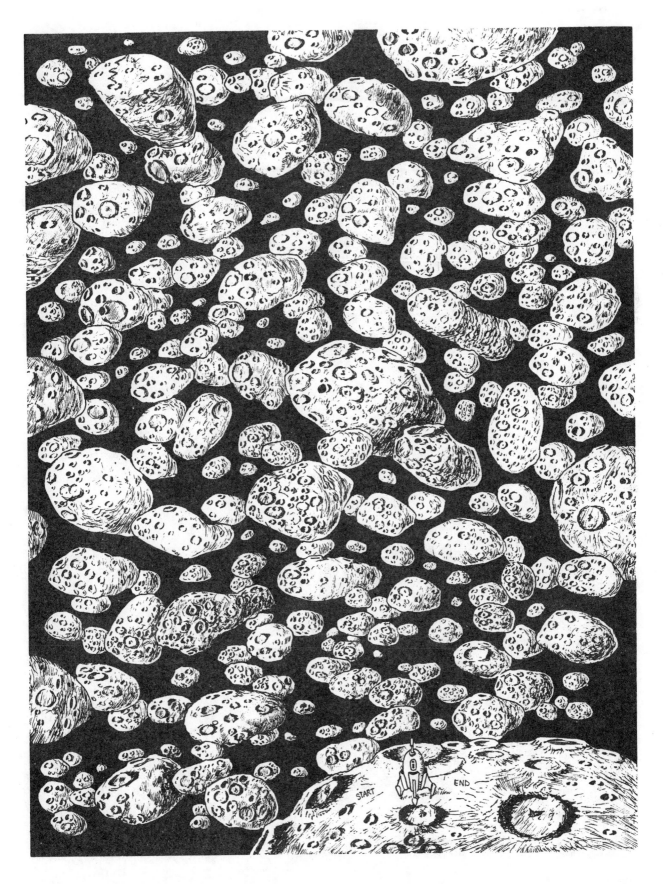

Tour of Jupiter

This planet is covered with turbulent clouds. Stay in the white clouds and find your way across Jupiter's surface.

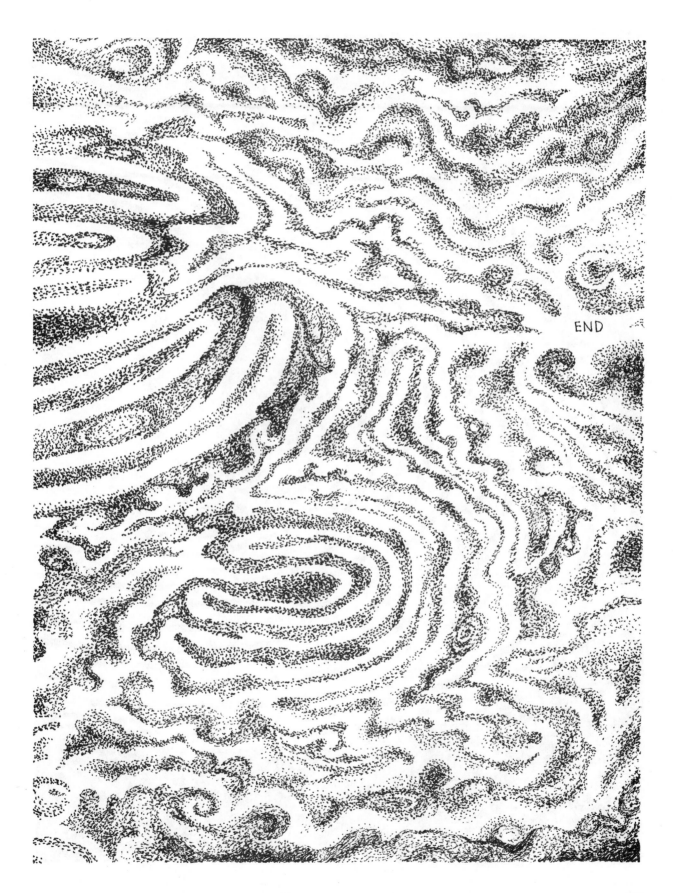

Tour of Saturn

Find your way around the rings of Saturn. Do not cross the dark areas.

Uranus, Neptune, and Pluto

Little is known about Uranus, Neptune, and Pluto. You will only be doing a flyby. On

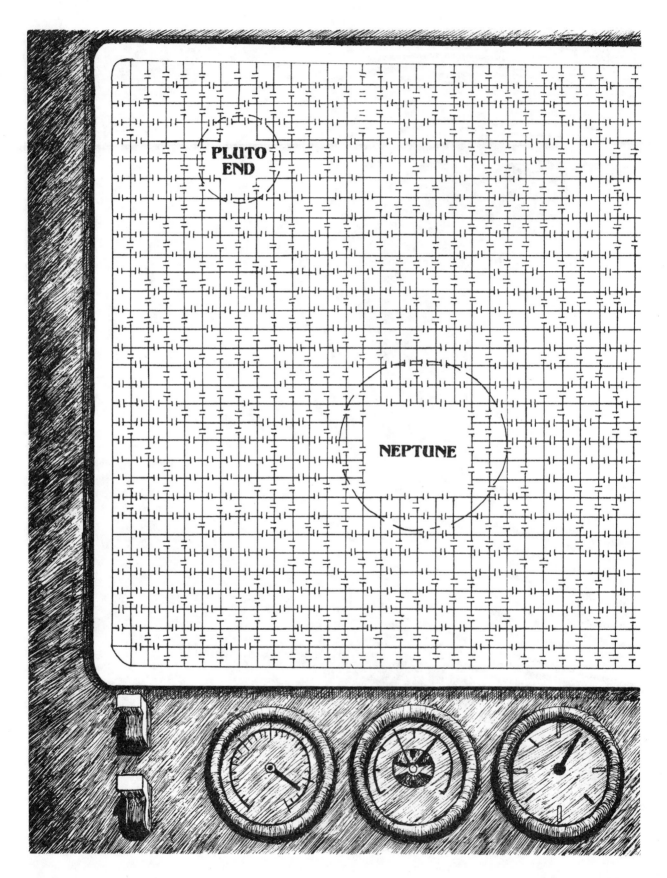

your computer screen, find a path through the openings to each planet in the order of their distance from the sun.

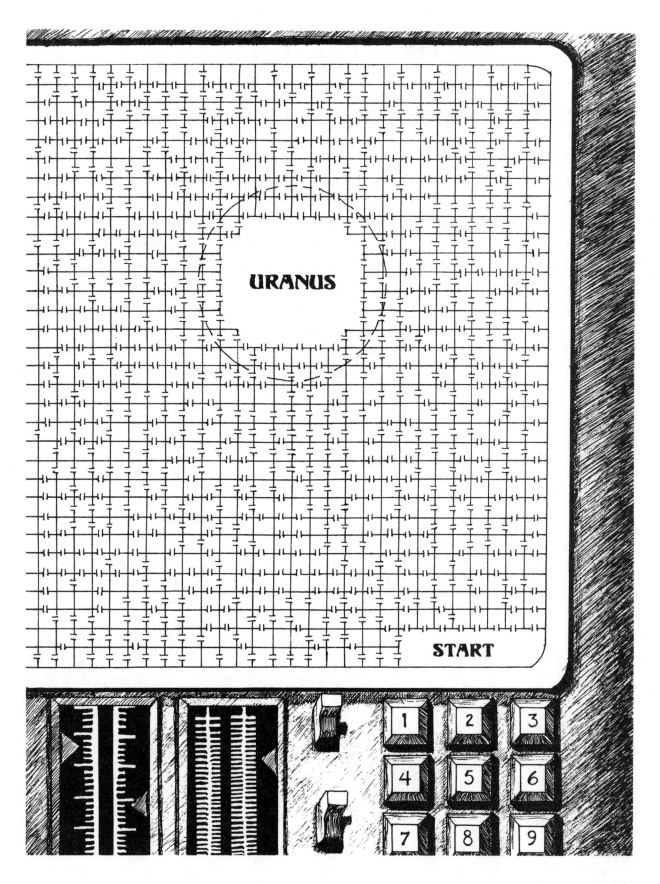

THE UNIVERSE

The size of the universe is almost beyond understanding. Distances are so great they are measured in light-years, the distance light travels in one year. Light travels 186,000 miles (300,000 kilometers) in one second. It takes light from our Sun 8 minutes to reach Earth, and 5 hours to reach Pluto. One of the closest stars to our solar system is Alpha Centauri, and it takes that star's light 4 years, 4 months to reach Earth. It is 4.3 light-years away.

There are many other interesting features in the universe, such as gas formations called nebulae, star clusters, and black holes. In addition, astronomers have recently found planets that revolve around other suns. Could they contain life? Your plan is to visit some of these features and planets.

Because of the immensity of the universe, it will be necessary for your space cruiser to reach speeds way beyond that of light for you to get home in a reasonable time. Fortunately, your spaceship is capable of such speed. So, get ready for the thrill of a lifetime.

Trip to Andromeda

Reach the Andromeda Galaxy by traveling on the connecting star beams.

Planet with Life

This planet appears to have life on it. Is it friendly life? You'd better not take any chances. Take a clear path while touring the planet and returning to the spaceship.

Horsehead and Orion Nebulae

Try to find a way on the space gases from the Horsehead Nebula to the Orion Nebula.

Exploding Star

The star you have just visited has exploded. You have only seconds to escape. Find your way on the bursting sun particles.

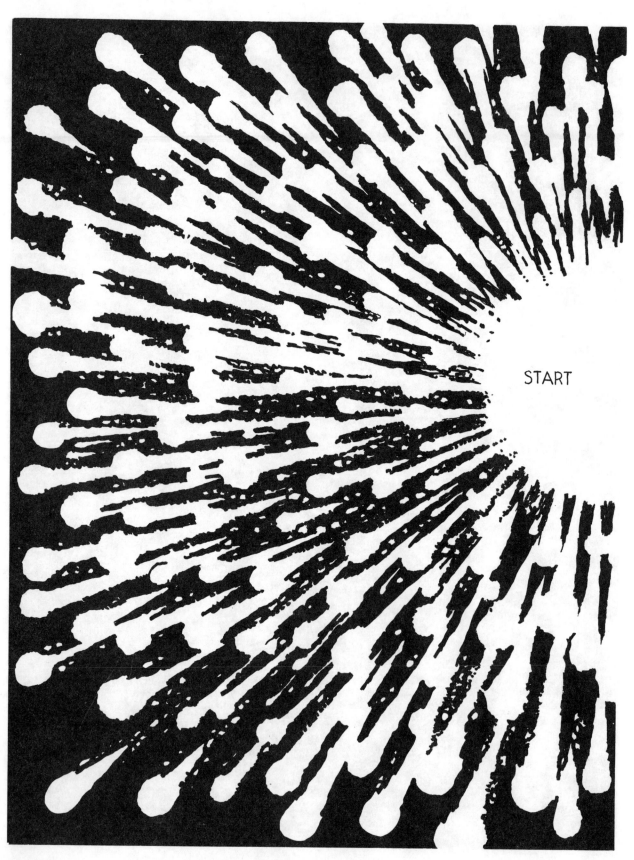

START

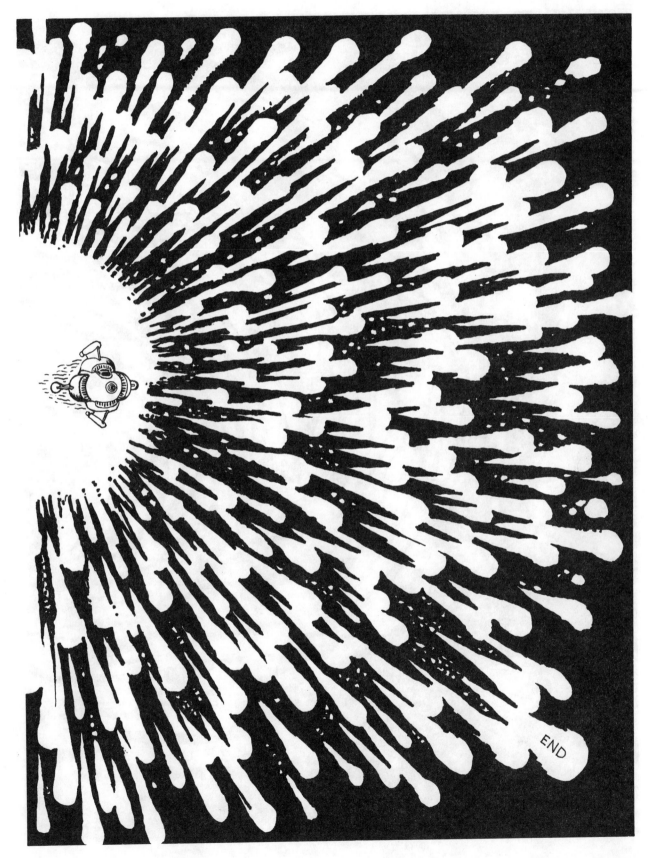

END

Tour of a Black Hole

The gravity from this black hole is pulling everything into it. Take a tour by finding a path on the white star matter, and be careful not to get pulled in.

Spiral Galaxies

Tour this field of spiral galaxies. You must visit the center of each galaxy only once. Stay only on the white areas, and do not backtrack.

Returning Home

Find your way home by returning to our solar system. Head back the way you came, and visit each of the features in the Universe as you return.

CONGRATULATIONS

You have been the first person to explore the solar system and universe. The information you have discovered and brought back to the scientific world is of great value. It will be studied for years to come. You have seen sights, explored worlds, and traveled distances that no one has ever accomplished before.

Also of great importance is the fact that you did not give up. You were summoned to take part in an important mission, and you met the challenge. You persevered at times when it would have been easy just to quit. For this, you will be ranked among the great astronauts.

Space Guides

If you had any trouble along the way, refer to the guides on the following pages for help.

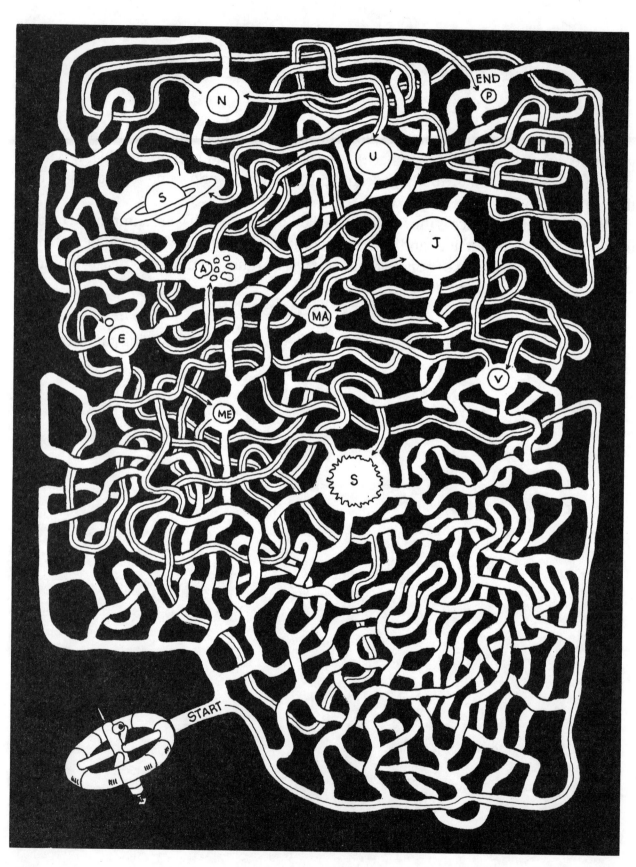

Space Shuttle

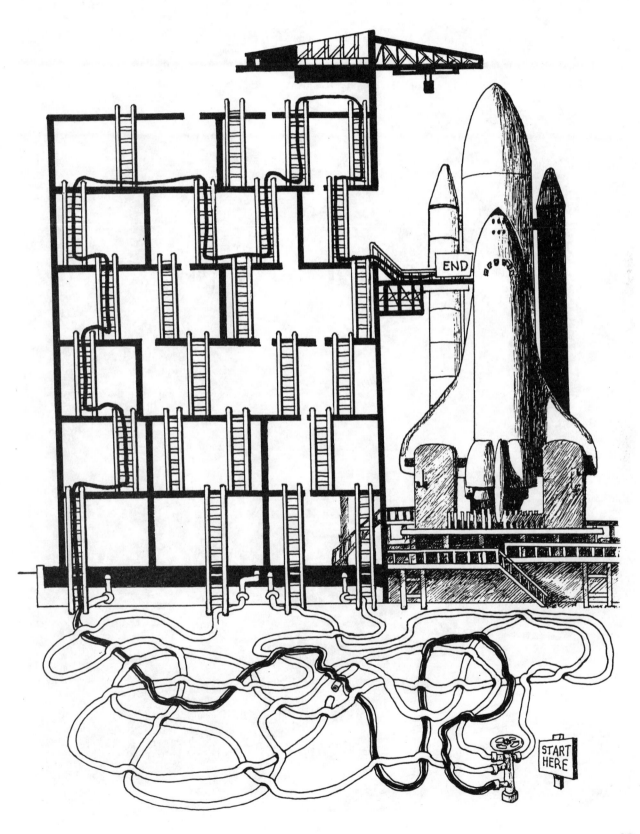

Space Station

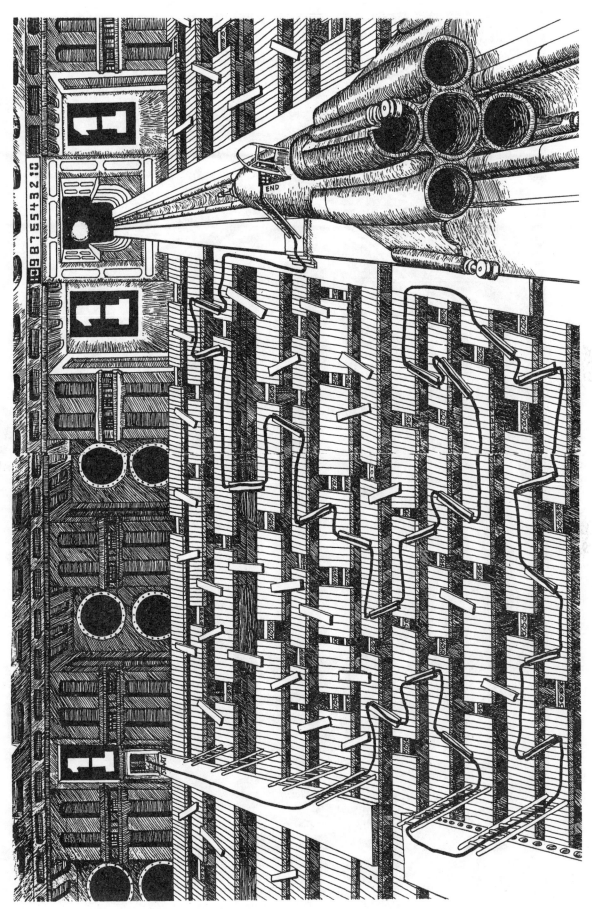

Departure

51

Tour of the Sun

Tour of Mercury

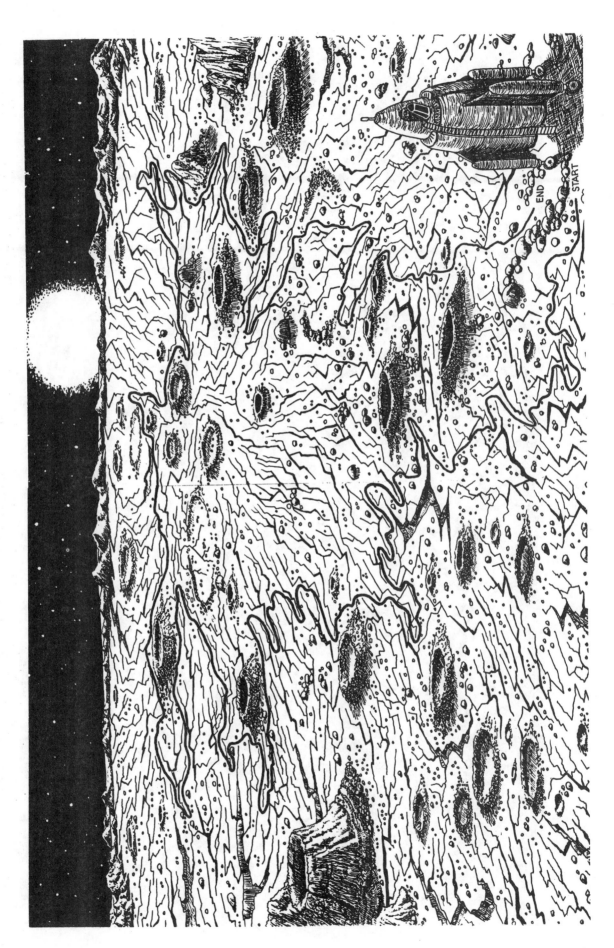

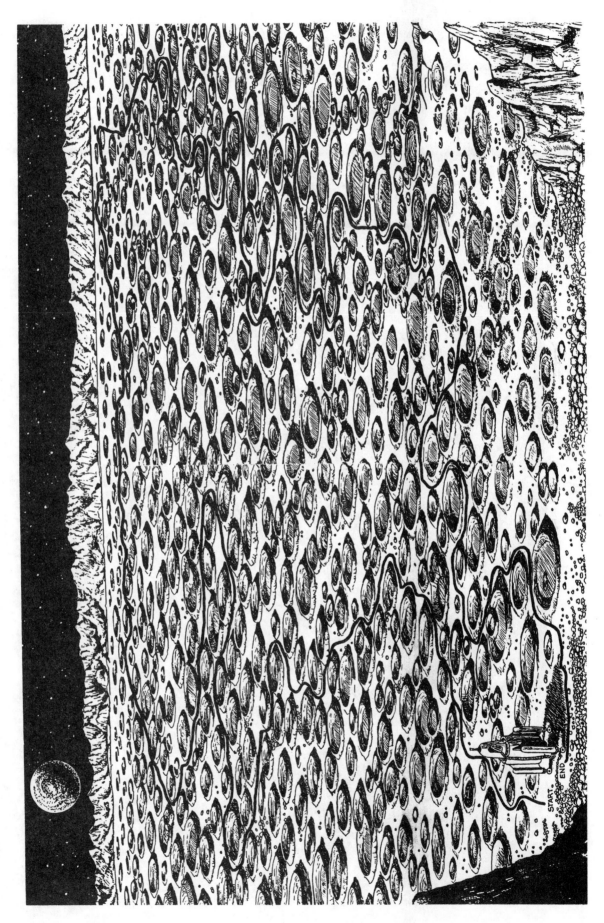

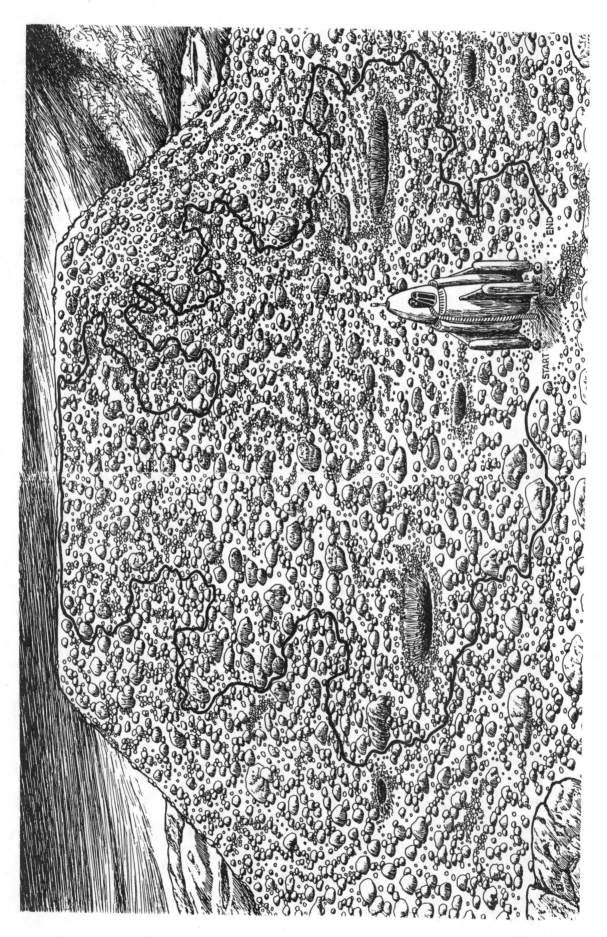

Asteroids

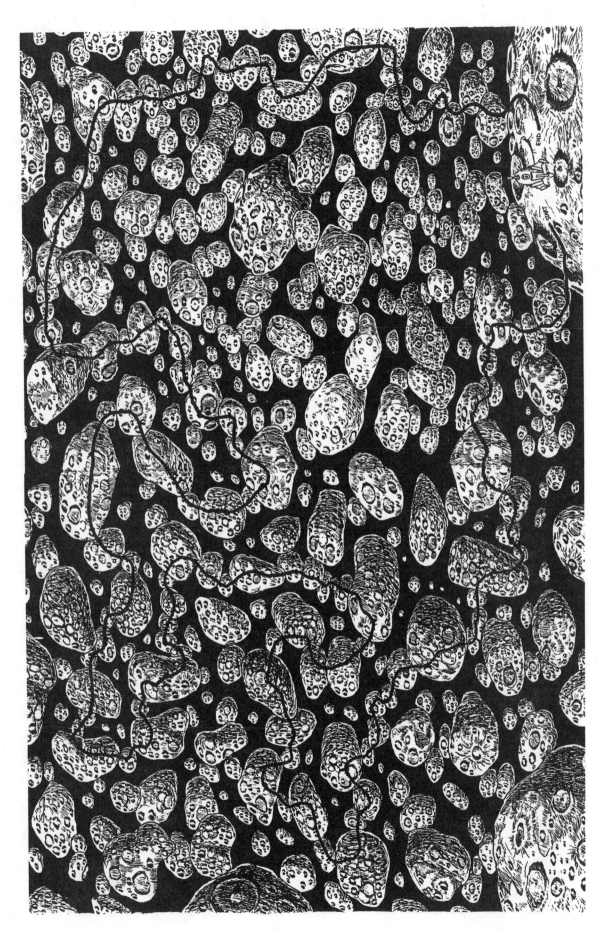

Tour of Jupiter

END

START

58

Tour of Saturn

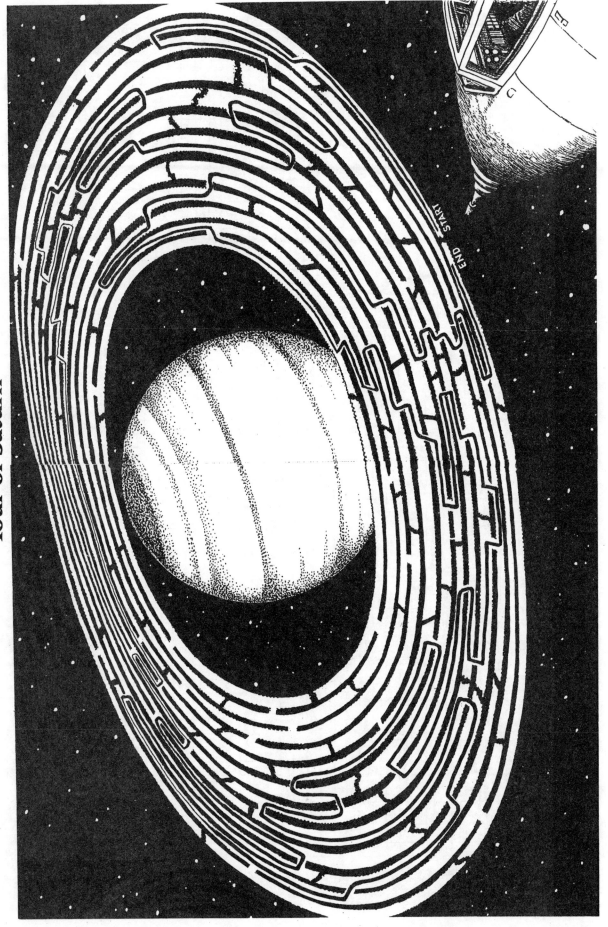

Uranus, Neptune, and Pluto

Trip to Andromeda

Planet with Life

Horsehead and Orion Nebulae

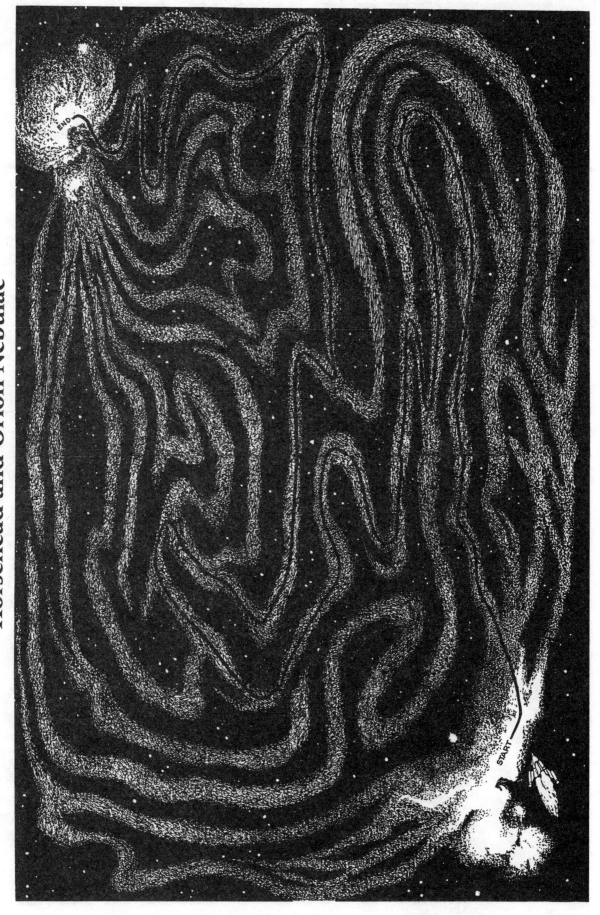

Exploding Star

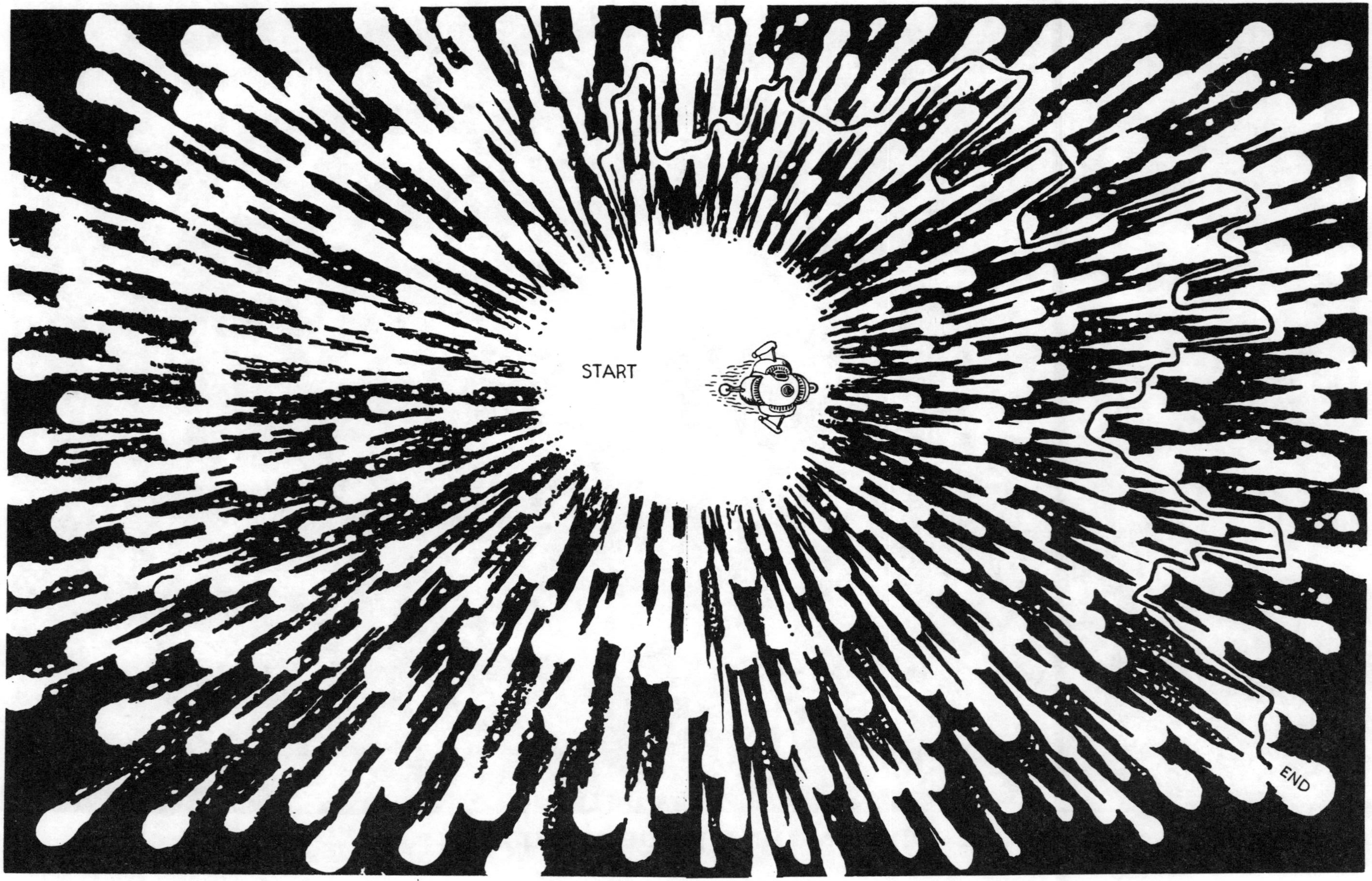

START

END

Tour of a Black Hole

Spiral Galaxies

Returning Home

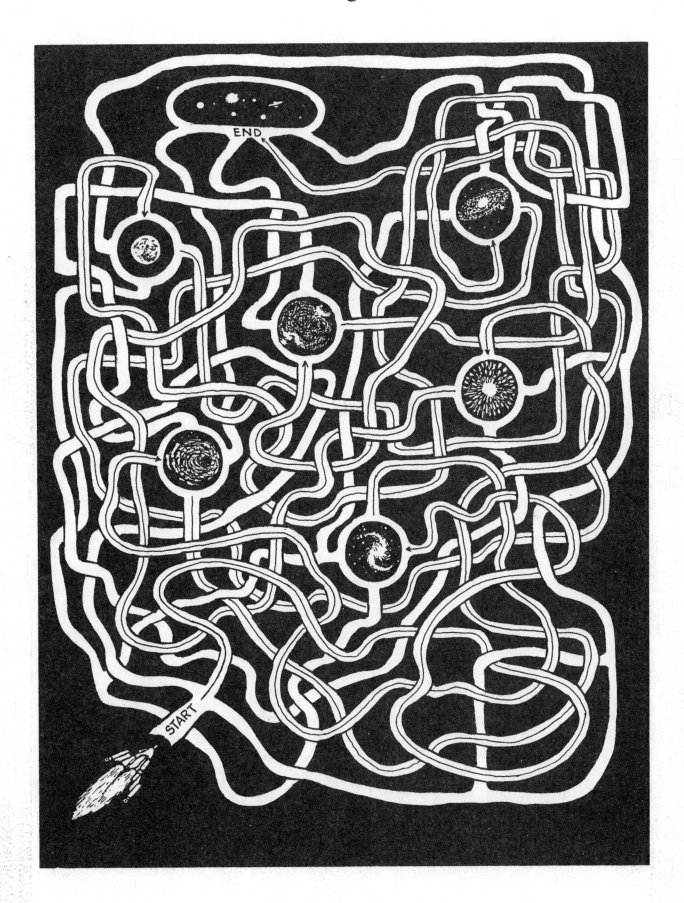

GREAT EXPLORER
MAZES

Roger Moreau

Contents

INTRODUCTION

The urge to explore and discover began with the very first people. These explorers probably went forth when they began to wonder what was on the other side of the hill, beyond the mountain range, or around the river bend. This urge has taken man from ocean to ocean, continent to continent, and now into space. It is a fascinating and exciting story that began long ago, goes on today, and will continue.

What is known as the Great Age of Discovery began in the 1400s, when countries in Europe desired to make money by trading with the Indies. When the Turks blocked popular Eastern trade routes after 1453, Europeans set out to find new routes. They had newer, faster, and more seaworthy ships that could hold greater loads than earlier ships, so, over the next 200 years, they sailed on the oceans, discovering and exploring new lands and finding new routes. During that time they found out more about the world than had ever been known before.

Many explorers were away from home for years. They suffered greatly and sometimes gave their lives. Their efforts required uncommon courage, strength, determination, and perseverance. They sometimes experienced the joy of victory, and too often suffered great defeat. The successful explorers had to be men of unselfish character who had complete dedication to their quests.

On the following pages you will have a chance to learn about many great explorers and follow in their footsteps. The way will not be easy. It will take courage, determination, and perseverance on your part to be successful. Even though you will face danger, sacrificing your life will, fortunately, never be required.

Now, boldly go forth . . . as they did. Good luck!

Roger Moreau

EARLY EXPLORERS

Marco Polo was an Italian explorer who explored central Asia and China between 1271 and 1292. He helped bring unknown information about the Orient back to Europe. He also made friends with the famous Mongol conqueror Kublai Khan, who gave Polo many gifts. Now, you have to reach Kublai Khan's camp **(page 75)**. Find a clear path. You can go up and down ladders and through tower openings when you travel on the Great Wall of China.

Christopher Columbus set sail from Spain on August 3, 1492, hoping to find a new route to the East by sailing west. His fleet consisted of three ships: the *Santa María*, the *Pinta,* and the *Niña.* They were sailing into unknown waters, and the three ships were greatly affected by the wind and currents. Finally, on October 12, 1492, Columbus sighted land, an island he named San Salvador. Now, *you* have to stay within the wind and current lines as you retrace Columbus's route **(pages 76 and 77)**. You must visit every island, and you cannot sail back over your own route.

The Portuguese explorer *Vasco da Gama* because the first person to sail around the Cape of Good Hope to India, in May 1498. When he returned with a cargo of spice, the king promoted him to the rank of Admiral of the Sea of India. See if you can bring back spices from India like da Gama **(page 78)**. There are many dangers. Find a clear path. If you're successful, maybe you'll also get a promotion.

Francisco Vásquez de Coronado was a Spaniard who explored the American Southwest in 1540. He was in search of the Seven Cities of Cibola and hoped to find gold. Instead, he discovered many ancient Indian dwellings, the Continental Divide, and the Grand Canyon. In this maze **(page 79)**, climb the ladders to reach the cliff dwellings.

When Coronado entered this dwelling **(pages 80 and 81)**, he was sure he'd find gold. You were probably expecting to, also. Sorry! Be careful not to disturb the tarantulas as you find a clear and fast exit to the right.

Henry Hudson was a British sea captain who hoped to find a passage to the Far East by sailing around North America. He explored the northeast coast of America and on his fourth voyage, in 1610, entered Hudson Bay. In this maze **(page 82)**, you have to try to find a way, by ship, to get to Hudson Bay. Use this map. It was drawn by one of Hudson's sailors who, unfortunately, was seasick when he drew it.

James Cook was a British mariner, who made many voyages exploring and mapping the regions in the South Pacific Ocean. On his first voyage there in 1768, he sailed around Cape Horn and reached New Zealand, where he mapped the North and South Islands. Rounding Cape Horn is no simple task, as you will see **(page 83)**. The winds are harsh and the waves high. Find your way between the waves to reach the Pacific.

Great Wall of China

To reach Kublai Khan's camp, navigate a clear path on and around the Great Wall of China. You can go up and down ladders and through tower openings.

San Salvador Island

To retrace Christopher Columbus's route to San Salvador Island, make sure you stay

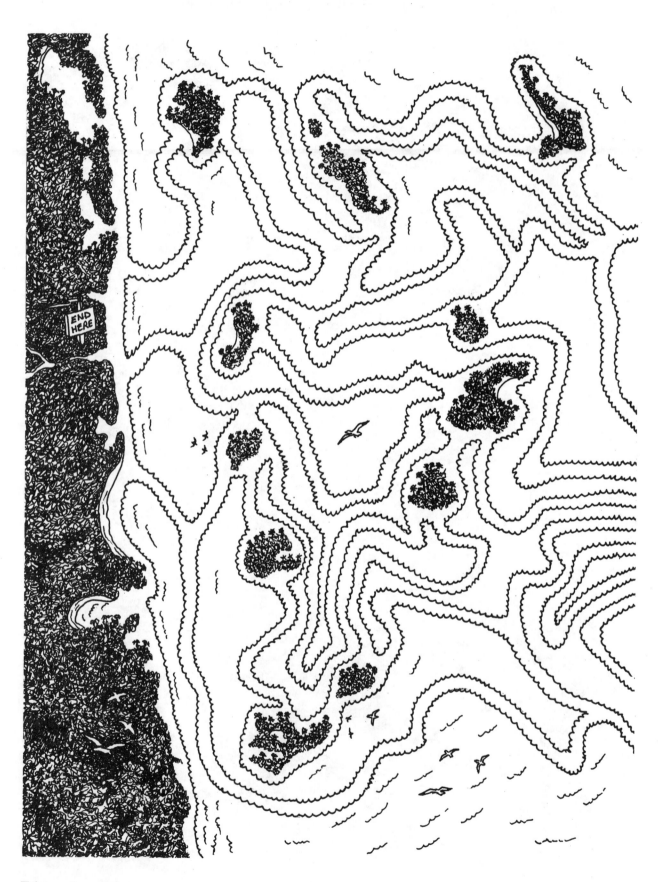

within the wind and current lines, that you visit every island, and that you do not sail back over your own route.

India Spice Shop

To reach the Spice Shop of India, you must find a clear path past the animals and other hazards and over the openings in the earth.

Indian Cliff Dwellings

To reach the ancient Indian cliff dwellings, climb the ladders.

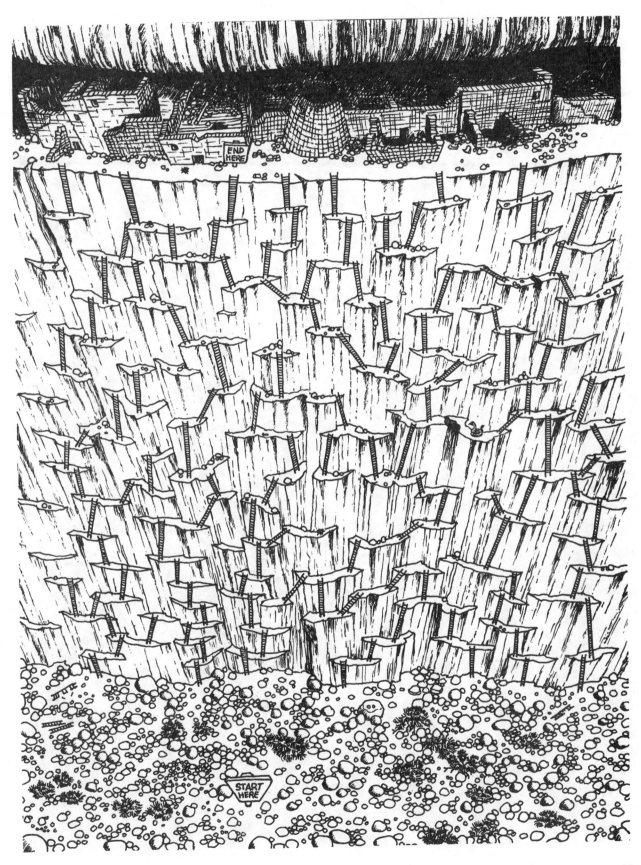

Inside an Indian Cliff Dwelling

There is no gold in this cliff dwelling, only tarantulas. To reach the exit, find a path through them.

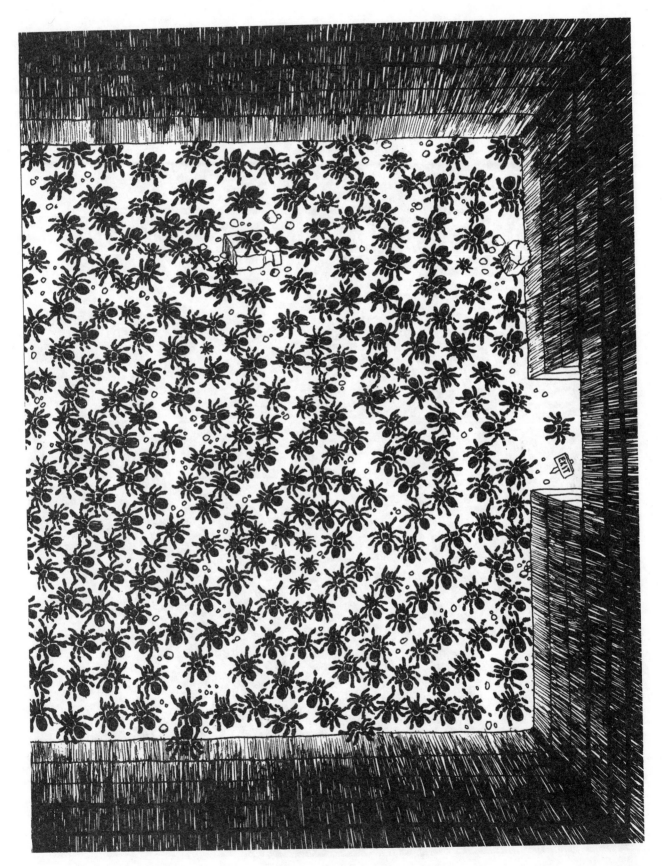

Hudson Bay

To sail to Hudson Bay, find the right tributary.

Cape Horn

To round Cape Horn and reach the Pacific Ocean, you must find your way between the waves.

19TH-CENTURY EXPLORERS

For many years, starting as early as the 1500s, explorers attempted unsuccessfully to find a Northwest Passage. *John Franklin* was a British naval explorer who made three attempts in the early 1800s. On his third expedition, in 1821, while Franklin was attempting to map the Arctic coastline, tragedy struck. An early winter set in and all of the expedition perished. In this maze **(page 85)**, you must find your way up the Hood River to Coronation Gulf, which is choked with blocks of ice. Find your way through the ice to reach Kent Peninsula. A herd of caribou is passing through the area, so avoid the places on the river where they block the way. Try to get through before winter sets in.

In May 1804, *Meriwether Lewis* and *William Clark* set out to travel up the Missouri River in an effort to find and map a way to the Pacific Ocean. Their journey took two years and covered 8,000 miles round-trip. Finding their way wasn't easy. They got help from an Indian woman named Sacagawea, who served as a guide and interpreter during their westward march in Shoshone Indian country. On **pages 86 and 87**, you must find your way up the Missouri River, and then up eastward-flowing streams to the Continental Divide—the area that extends south-southeast from northwest Canada to South America. Next, find the right trail that will enable you to discover a westward-flowing stream that will take you to the mighty Columbia River and the Pacific Ocean. You won't have Sacagawea to help you, but you will have an old Indian map.

During the mid-19th century, a great effort was made in Africa to find the head-waters of the Nile River. In 1858, two British explorers, *Richard Burton* and *John Hanning Speke*, discovered Lake Victoria and suggested that it might be the source of the White Nile. In 1866, *David Livingstone,* a Scottish medical missionary, set out to find the source of the White Nile and was not heard from for several years. In 1869, a British reporter named *Henry Stanley* set out to find Livingstone. He found him at Lake Tanganyika, which had been discovered by Burton and Speke in 1858. When he first saw Livingstone, he uttered those famous words, "Dr. Livingstone, I presume?" See if you can find your way up the White Nile to Lake Victoria **(pages 88 and 89)**. You must row upstream to the falls and then hike around any falls to get into the streams above them. You can go up and down the streams, but you cannot row up any falls.

In 1860–1861, the Irishman *Robert O'Hara Burke* and his English companion, *William Wills,* became the first men to cross Australia from south to north. On the return trek, they died of starvation. Follow their route from Melbourne to the Gulf of Carpentaria **(pages 90 and 91)**. Find a clear path and take plenty of food and water.

Kent Peninsula

To find your way through the ice to reach Kent Peninsula, make sure you use a path that is not blocked by caribou.

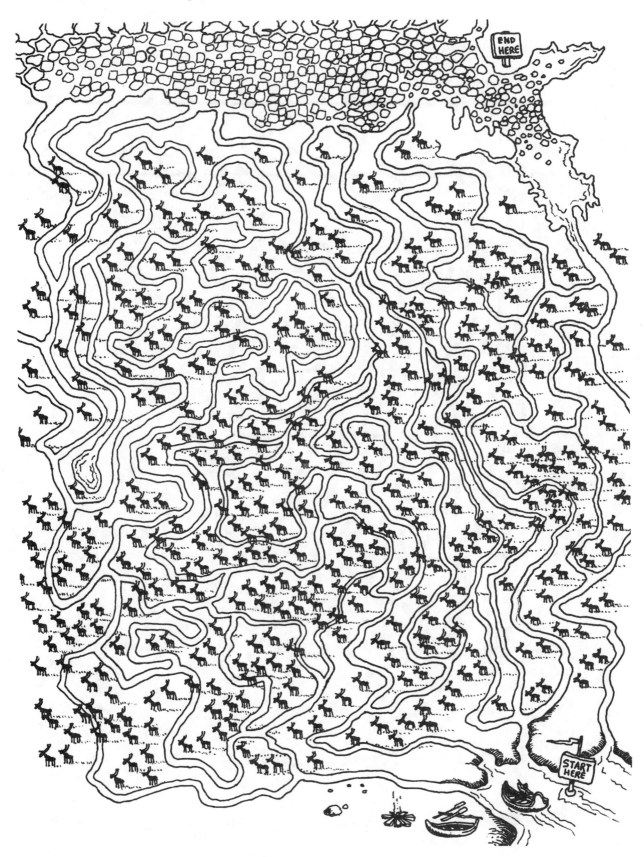

Missouri River

Your goal here is to find the correct path up the Missouri River to the Continental

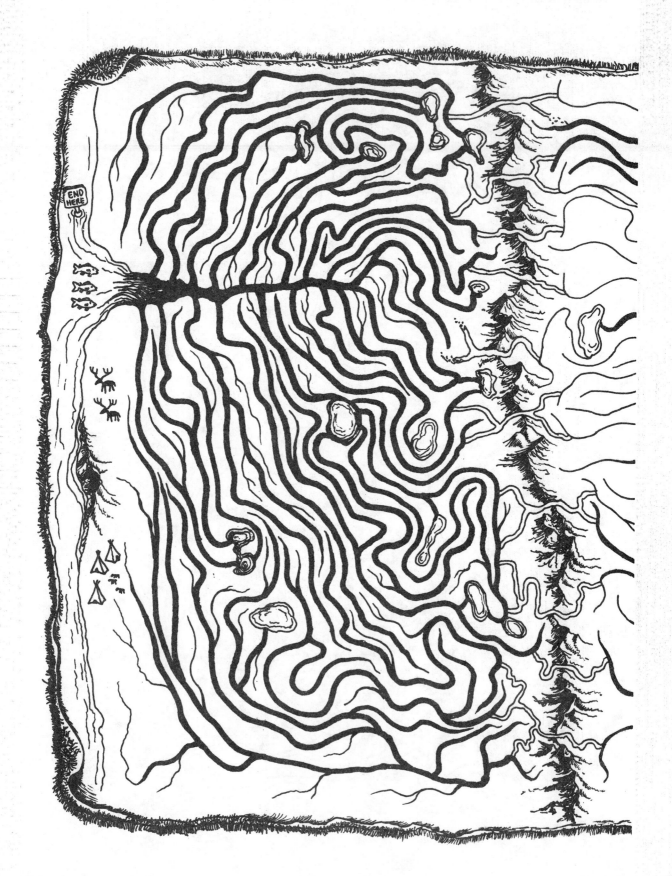

Divide, and then the trail that will take you from the Continental Divide to the Columbia River to the Pacific Ocean.

Lake Victoria

To get to Lake Victoria from the Nile River, find the correct stream to the falls, and the

END AT LAKE

correct path from the falls to the lake. Remember, you can move up and down the streams, but you cannot row up the falls.

Gulf of Carpentaria

To navigate the route from Melbourne to the Gulf of Carpentaria, find a path that avoids the wildlife and other hazards and crosses the openings in the earth.

20TH-CENTURY EXPLORERS

Commander Robert E. Peary was an American explorer who was the first man to reach the North Pole, on April 6, 1909. He trekked over drifting pack ice for 413 nautical miles. Now, you have to get to the North Pole **(page 93).** The ice is always cracking and moving. Avoid the cracks in the pack ice and keep dry. Now that you're there you must return **(page 94)**—a trip of 413 nautical miles. Note that the ice has changed. Good luck!

After Peary reached the North Pole, the race was on for the South Pole. Two explorers, *Roald Amundsen* of Norway and *Robert Falcon Scott* of Great Britain, were involved in the race between 1910 and 1912. Each went by a different route. The distance to the South Pole was about 900 miles. Amundsen reached the Pole first, on December 14, 1911. He left his tent there, which Scott found when he arrived a few months later. On the return trip, Scott and his four companions froze to death. Now, you must find a path to the Pole **(page 95).**

You made it! Now, you must get back—a trip of 900 miles **(page 96).** Is it possible?

Hiram Bingham was an American explorer who discovered Machu Picchu, an ancient Inca city 6,270 feet high in the Andes, in 1911. Follow his map to the ancient city **(page 97).** You can go under and on the overpasses.

Now, climb the steep trail to the city **(page 98).** It could be tough.

Howard Carter was an English archaeologist who discovered the undisturbed tomb of the pharaoh Tutankhamen in 1922. The opening was a stairway found under tons of rocks in the Valley of the Kings in Egypt. Find a clear path to the stairway **(page 99).** Now, explore the tomb and find King Tut **(p. 100 and 101).** Avoid the debris and snakes.

On July 20–21, 1969, the crew of Apollo 11—*Neil Armstrong, Edwin Aldrin, Jr.* and *Michael Collins*—broadcast to earth from the moon, "Houston, Tranquillity Base here. The 'Eagle' has landed." Then, as Neil Armstrong stepped from the lunar module footpad onto the moon, he announced, "That's one small step for a man, one giant leap for mankind." Man had finally set foot on the moon. Now, you have a chance to explore Tranquillity Base **(pages 102 and 103).** Do not step on or over any rocks or into any shadows.

In April 1912, the luxury ship *Titanic* struck an iceberg in the North Atlantic and went down with a loss of 1,522 people. On September 1, 1985, Robert Ballard found the *Titanic* 13,000 feet down on the ocean floor. See if you can find it in the maze **(page 104).** A grid has been placed over the search area. Move through the openings to try to find the *Titanic*.

Explore the *Titanic* **(page 105).** Find a clear path over the top surface of the ship.

In France, caves have been found with beautiful ancient paintings covering the walls. Now, you can discover one **(pages 106 and 107).** This is your chance to be included with the great explorers of the past. If you are successful at exploring your discovery, name the cave after yourself. But, remember, once you go in you have to be able to get out.

North Pole

To follow in the footsteps of Commander Robert Peary and reach the North Pole, find the correct path that avoids the cracks in the ice.

North Pole

Now that you've reached the North Pole, you must find your way back.

South Pole

Now, try your luck at finding the South Pole. Once again, avoid the cracks in the ice.

South Pole

Now that you have reached the South Pole, you must find your way back.

Machu Picchu

To travel to the ancient Inca city of Machu Picchu, you have to go under and on the overpasses.

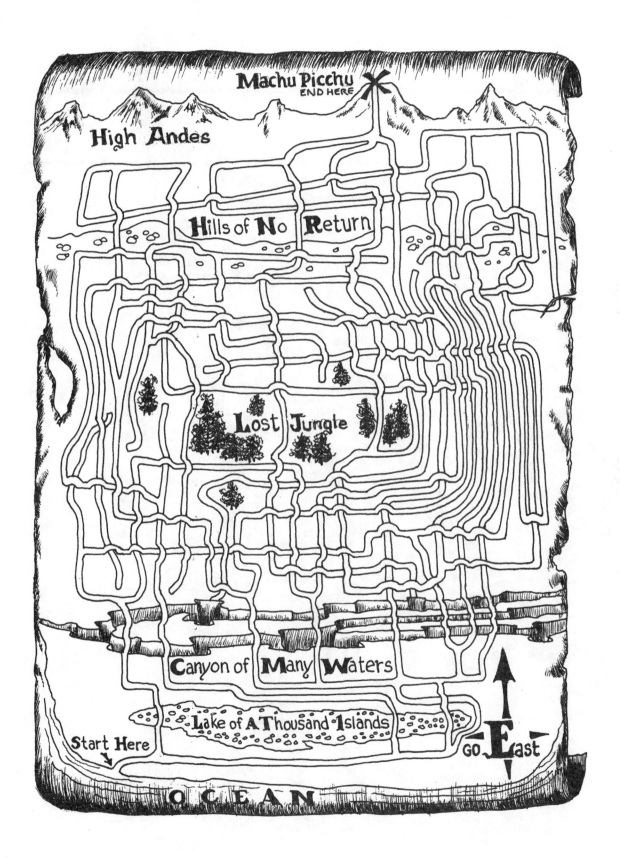

Machu Picchu

Now, climb the steep trail to the city.

Tomb of Tutankhamen

Find a path to the stairway that leads to the tomb of Tutankhamen.

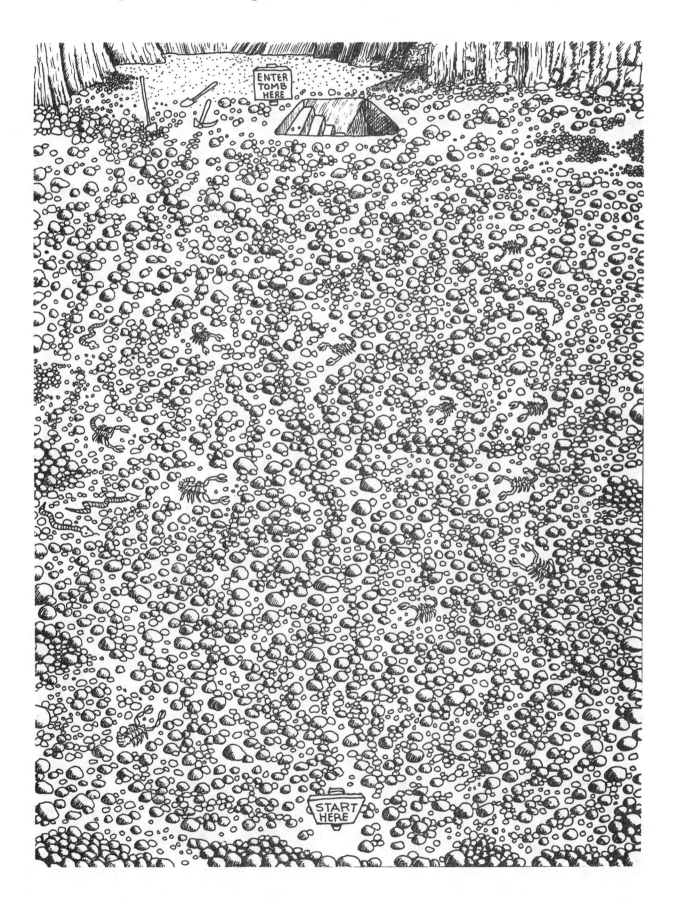

Tomb of Tutankhamen

Now that you're inside the tomb, find a path past the debris and snakes to find King Tut.

Tranquillity Base

Now that you've landed on the Moon, find a path around Tranquillity Base. Do not step on or over any rocks or into any shadows.

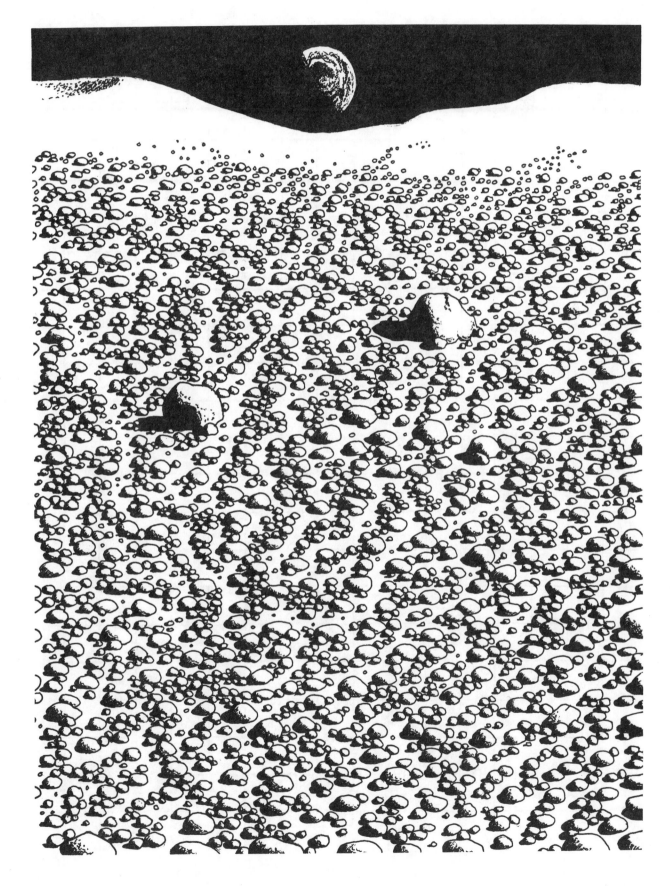

Titanic

To reach the *Titanic*, maneuver through the openings in the maze.

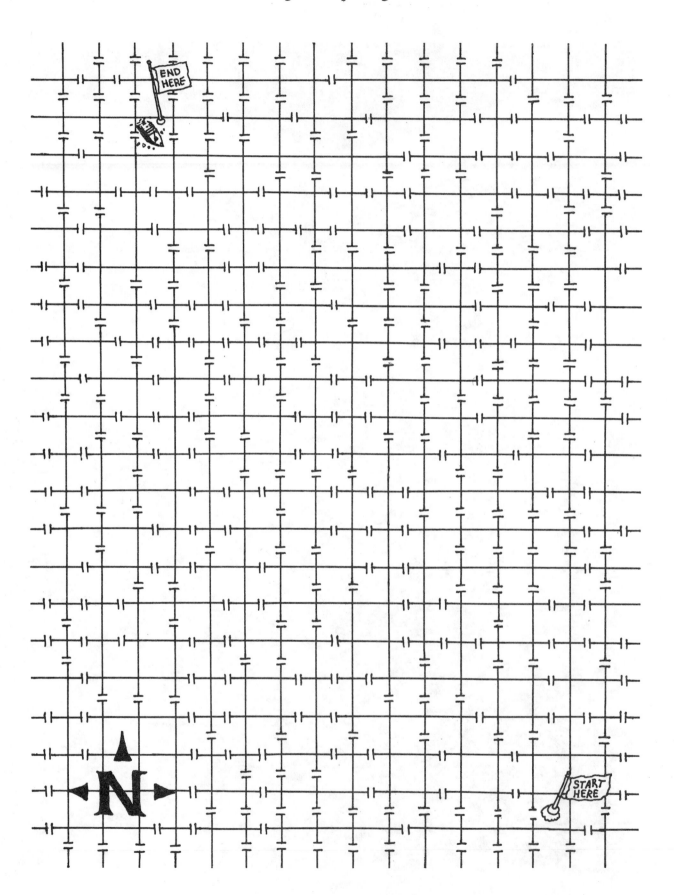

Titanic

Now that you've found the *Titanic*, explore it by traveling along a path on the top surface of the ship.

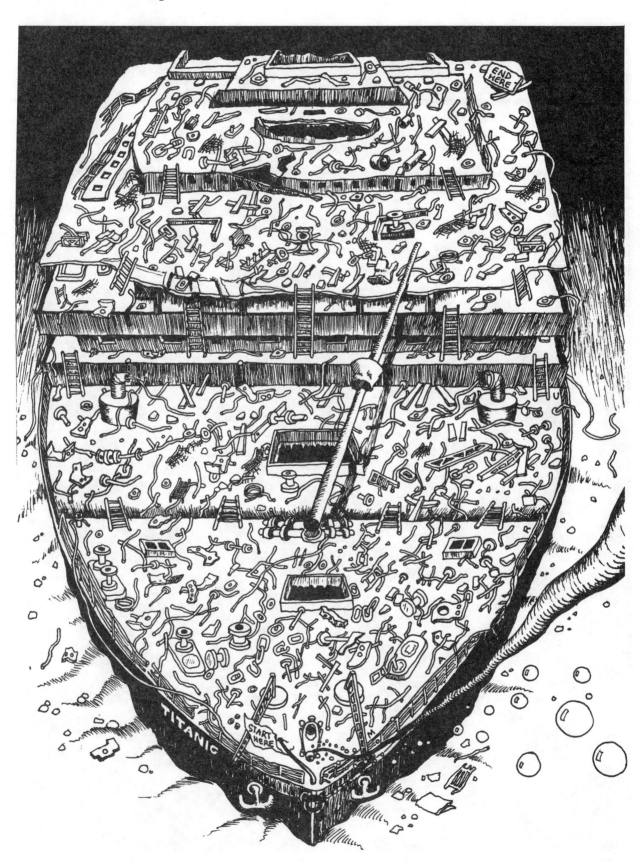

French Cave

Chart a path through this cave in the hopes of discovering ancient paintings.

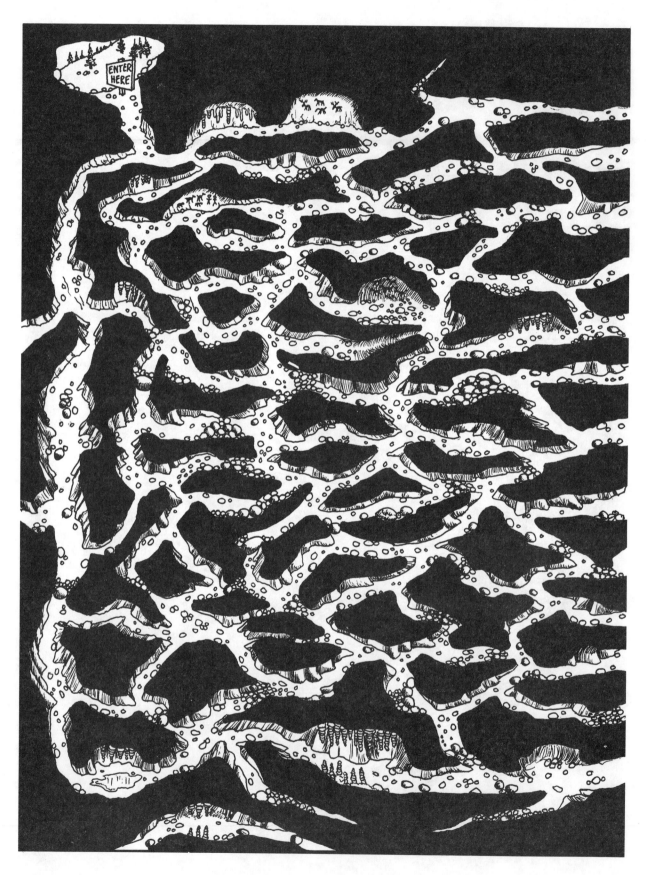

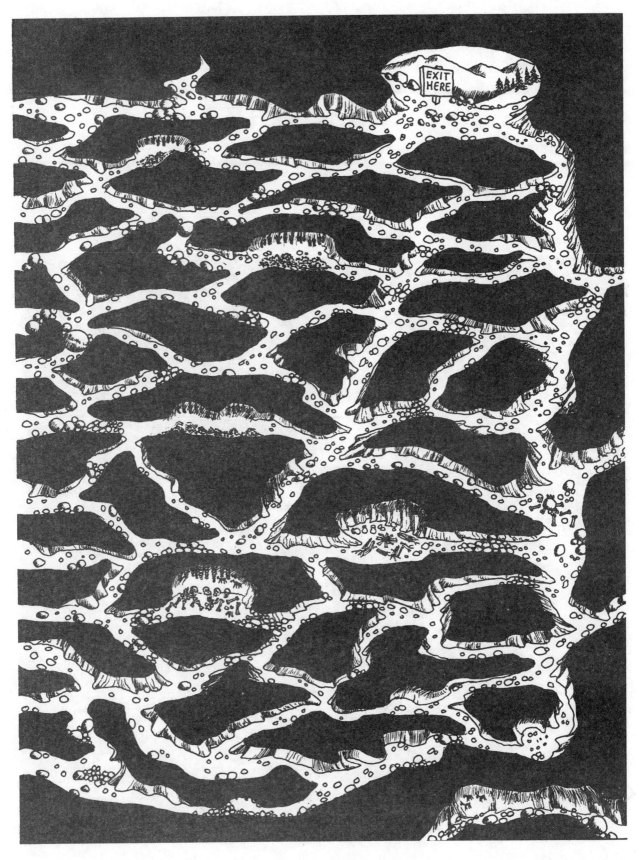

107

CONGRATULATIONS!

You have been successful in following in the footsteps of many of the great explorers of the past, and have learned how important it is not to get discouraged or give up. There is an exciting world out there for you to explore. Now, go forth with all the courage and determination of those past explorers and make your mark in whatever you choose to do. Remember, strive to know what is over the hill, beyond the mountain range, and around the bend in the river.

EXPLORER'S GUIDES

If you had any trouble finding your way through the mazes in this book, use the explorer's guides on the following pages. These guides should be used only in case of an emergency. The guide shown below is for the cover maze.

Great Wall of China

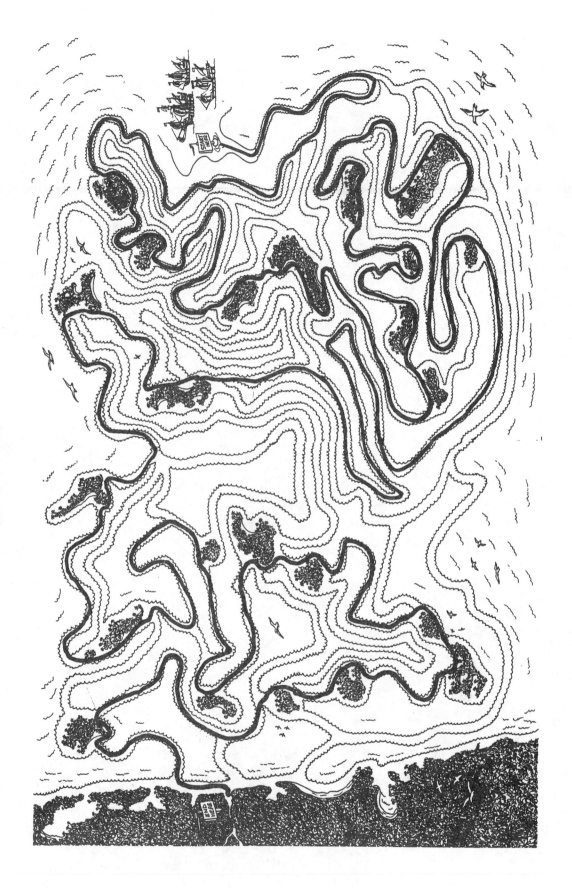

San Salvador Island

India Spice Shop

Indian Cliff Dwellings

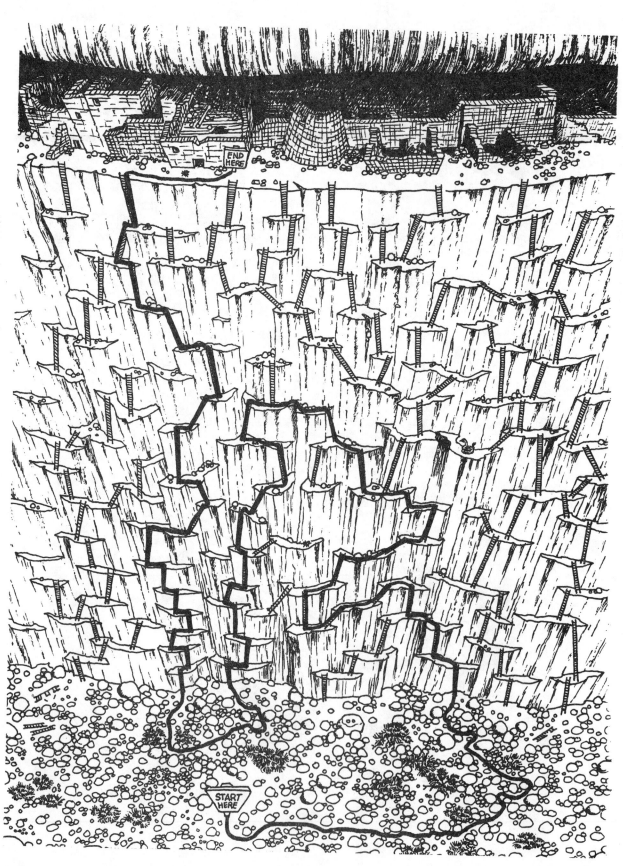

Inside an Indian Cliff Dwelling

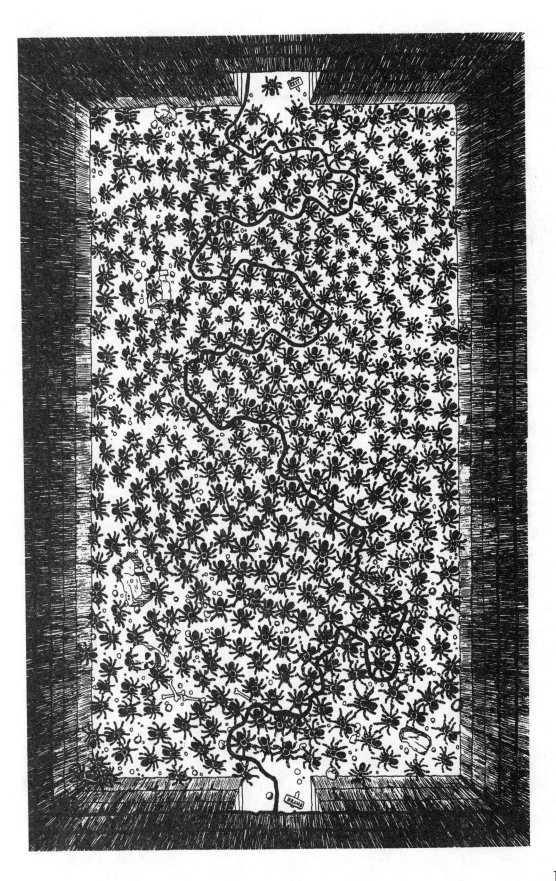

Hudson Bay

Cape Horn

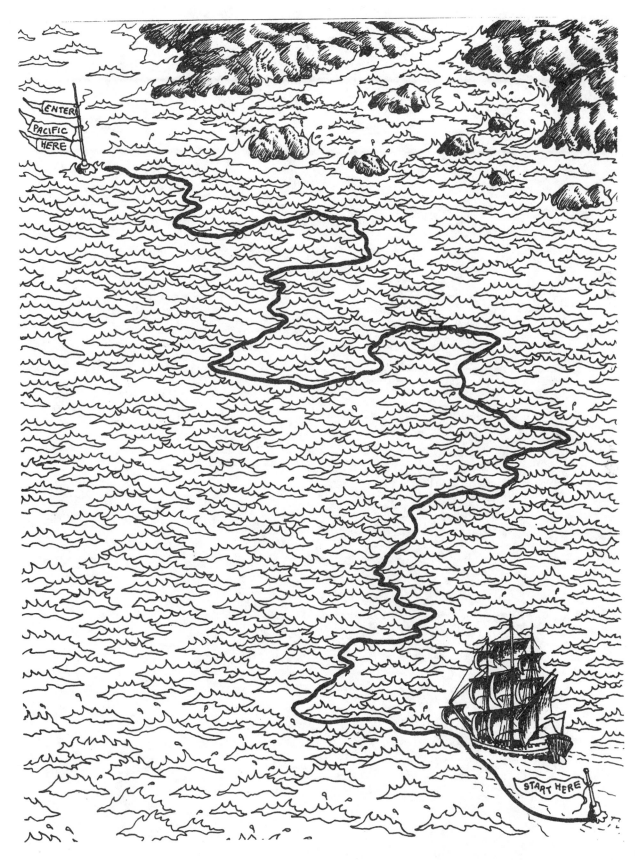

Kent Peninsula

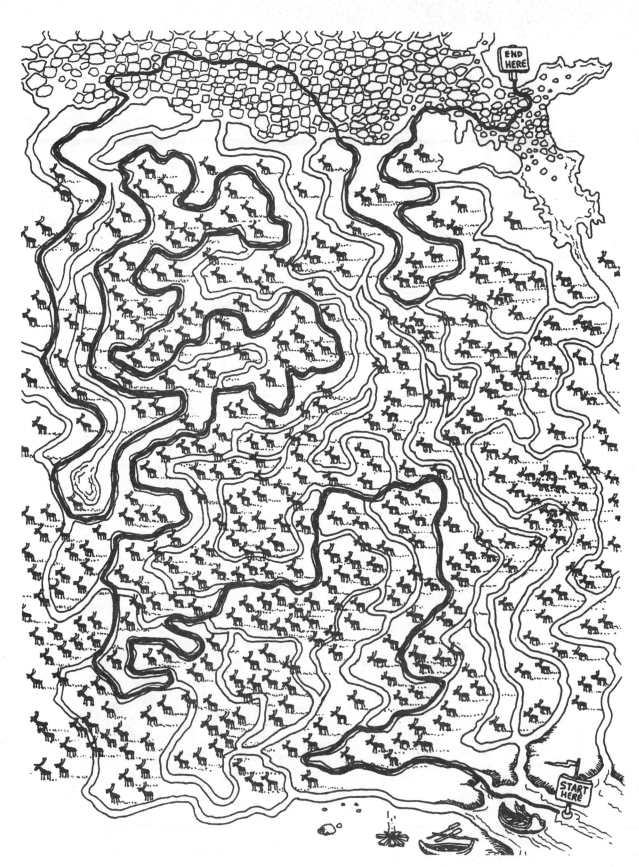

Missouri River

Lake Victoria

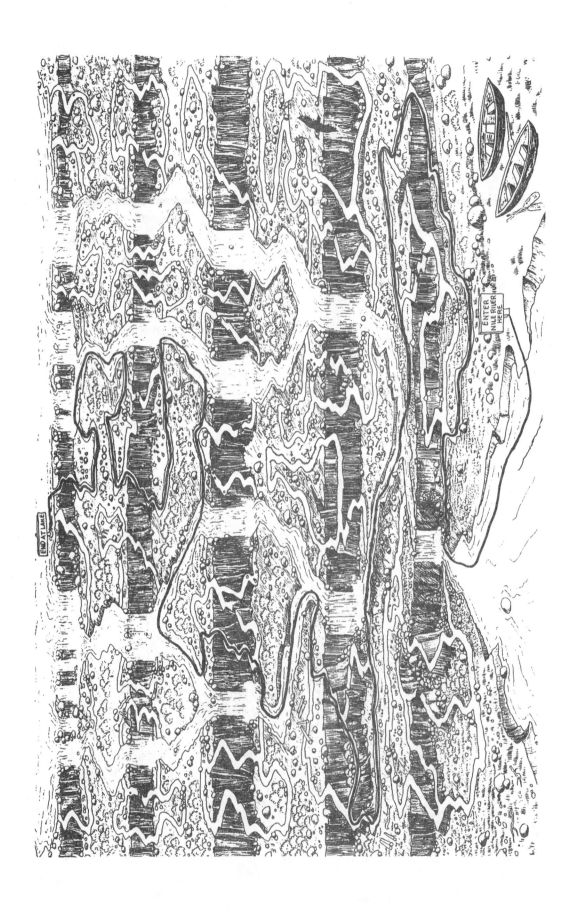

Gulf of Carpentaria

North Pole

North Pole

South Pole

Machu Picchu

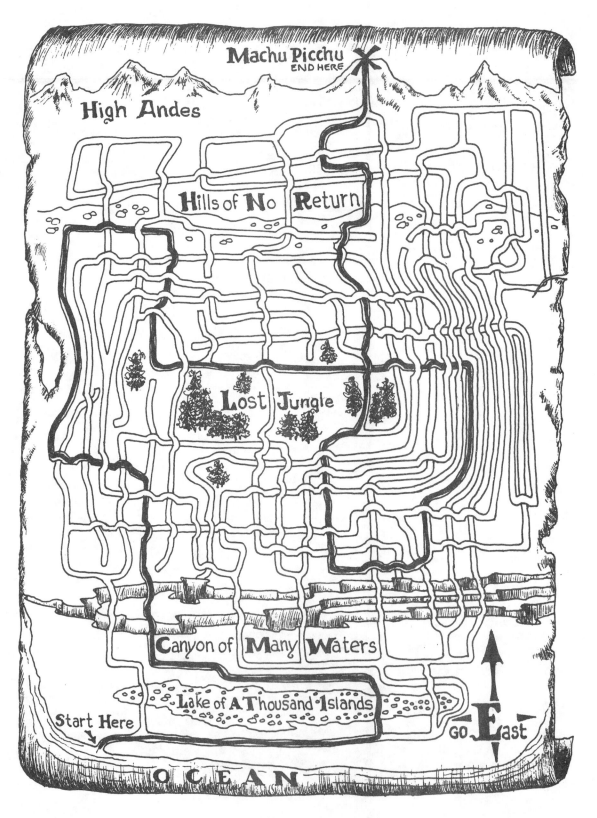

Machu Picchu

Tomb of Tutankhamen

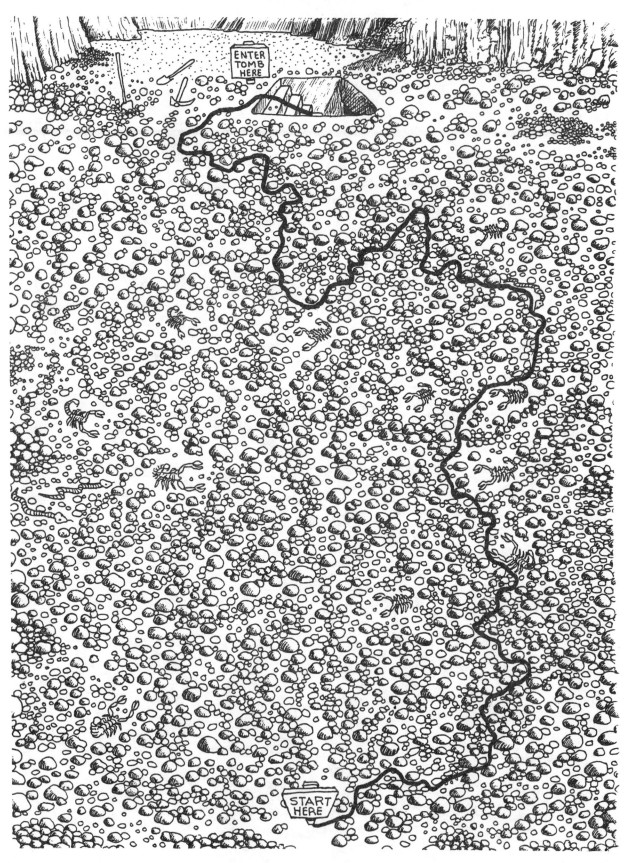

Tomb of Tutankhamen

Tranquility Base

Titanic

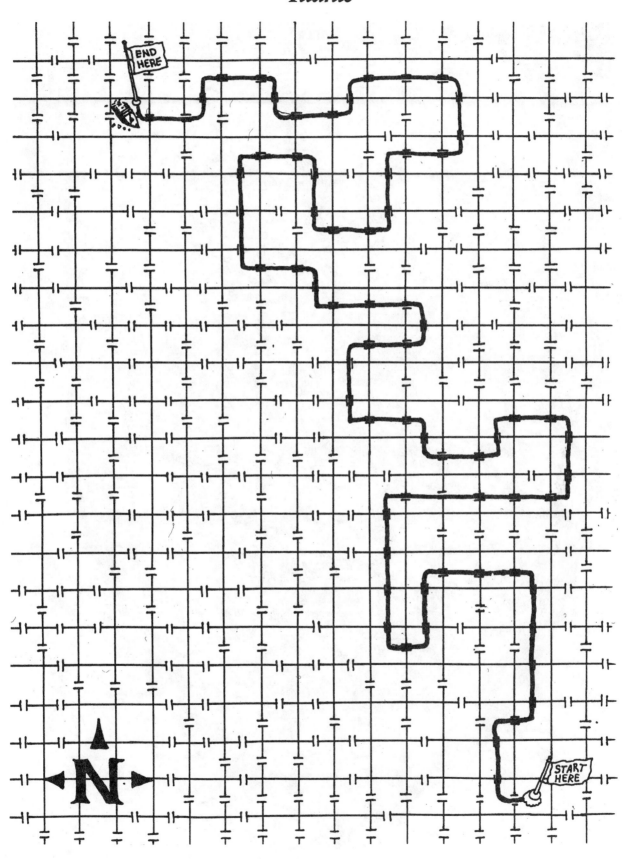

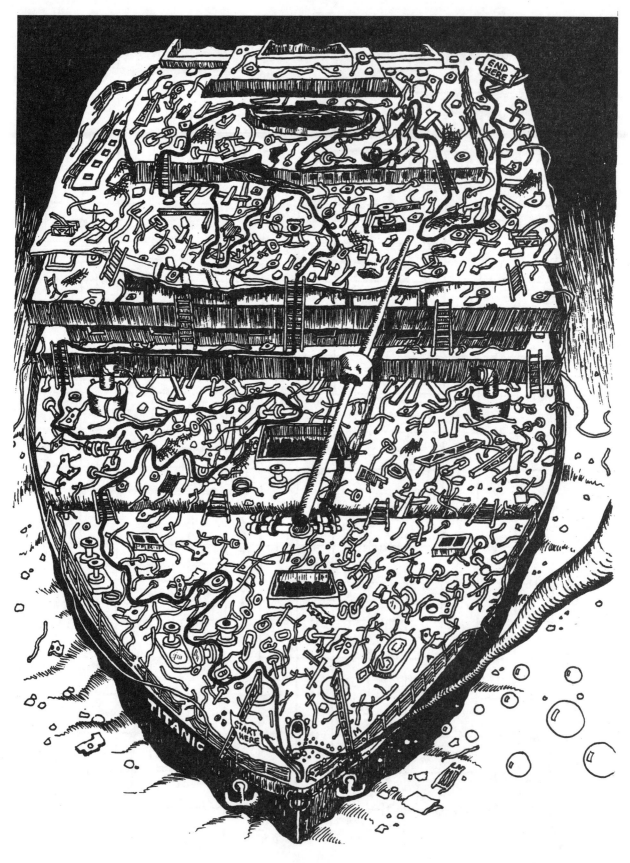

French Cave

SAVE THE EARTH
MAZE BOOK

Contents

Introduction

The great planet Earth we live on has in the past been called many names that have described its condition. They were friendly, healthy names like the "Good Earth" and "Mother Earth." We could take comfort in knowing that Earth could sustain us and provide for us. In recent times, however, our planet has taken on a new name, a name which is both depressing and frightening. It describes an Earth that is in grave danger, an Earth that may no longer be able to provide for or sustain us. The Earth of today is called the "Endangered Earth."

The Earth is in danger because of the negligence and carelessness of man. Such problems as air pollution, acid rain, water pollution, toxic waste, species extinction, fisheries depletion, deforestation, and radiation peril are just a few of the man-made problems. If something isn't done soon to end the mistreatment, it will be too late to save planet Earth.

On the following pages, you will learn about some of these problems; but of more importance, you will have a chance to do something about it. If you are successful, you could help in taking a great step toward saving Earth!

For practice start with the cover, where smoke from a careless fire is covering the sky. Carry the water through the jungle and up the mountain to put out the fire.

It will not be easy. Nothing worth having comes easily. So don't give up. Face each problem with courage and determination and when you succeed Mother Earth will thank you.

Oceans and Streams

Water pollution from acid rain, fertilizers, and urban runoff has affected our oceans and streams. Combined with overfishing and our altering of the natural flow of rivers, these man-made problems endanger wildlife and threaten the ecological balance. The mazes on the next few pages present some of these problems.

SAVE THE DOLPHIN

A dolphin is entangled in some rotting gill nets. You can save it by finding a clear pathway through the rotting nets and untangling it.

FREE THE FISHES

In this overfished area several fish are hooked and snagged on the bottom. They will die if you don't find a clear path down to them between the lines and hooks.

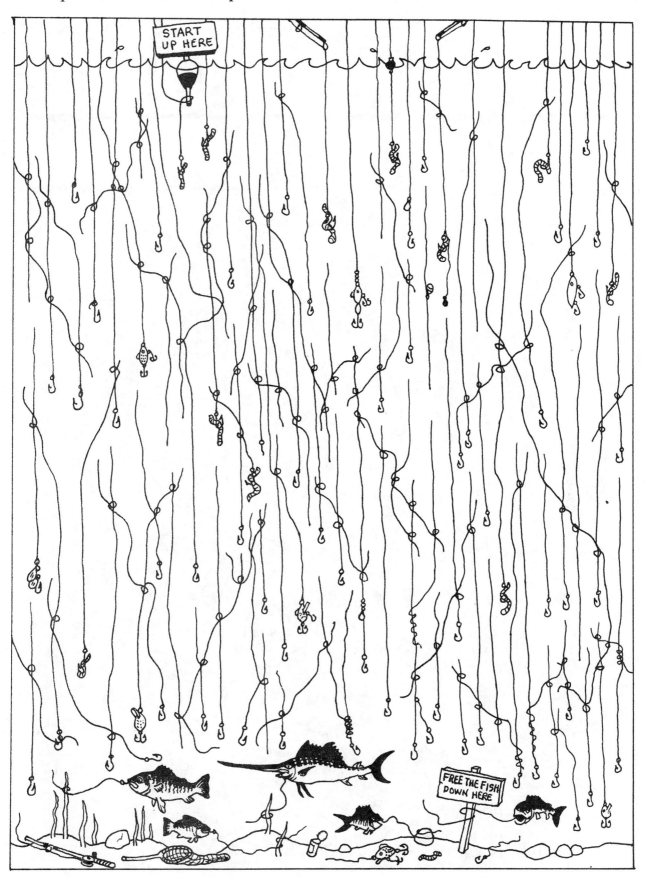

HELP THE SALMON

The river has been dammed many times. The dams confuse the salmon that want to

START HERE

return to where they were born to lay their eggs. Help them find a way around the dams to reach the stream.

FREE THE WHALE
This whale lost its way while migrating south. It turned into San Francisco Bay and

swam up the creeks that flow through the marshes at the back of the bay. Help him find his way back to the ocean.

PREVENT ATOMIC TESTING

This island in the South Pacific is to be sacrificed in an atomic test that will kill all

START HERE

wildlife, destroy the island, and pollute the ocean. Hurry up and find your way to the bomb and pull the fuse.

HELP THE TURTLE

Some turtles are almost extinct. This sea turtle, hatched from an egg on land, must get to the ocean to survive. Help him past the many predators that lie in wait for him.

Wildlife

Many species of wildlife throughout the world are endangered because of the carelessness of man and because of shrinking environments. Man must intervene and become actively involved to save some species. The following mazes present some of the problems and give you a chance to help.

HELP THE DUCK FAMILY

This mallard drake and hen want to return their young to the nest. Help them find a clear channel to the nest.

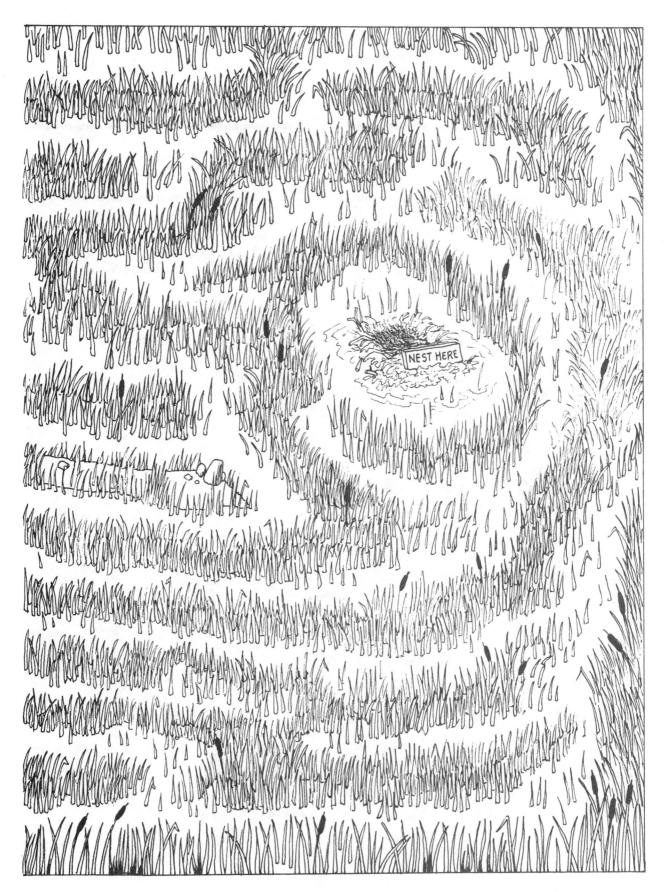

WATERPONDS FOR WATERFOWL

Migrating waterfowl need waterponds to feed and rest in. Waterponds across the country have been disappearing every year. This farmer will let you dig a waterpond

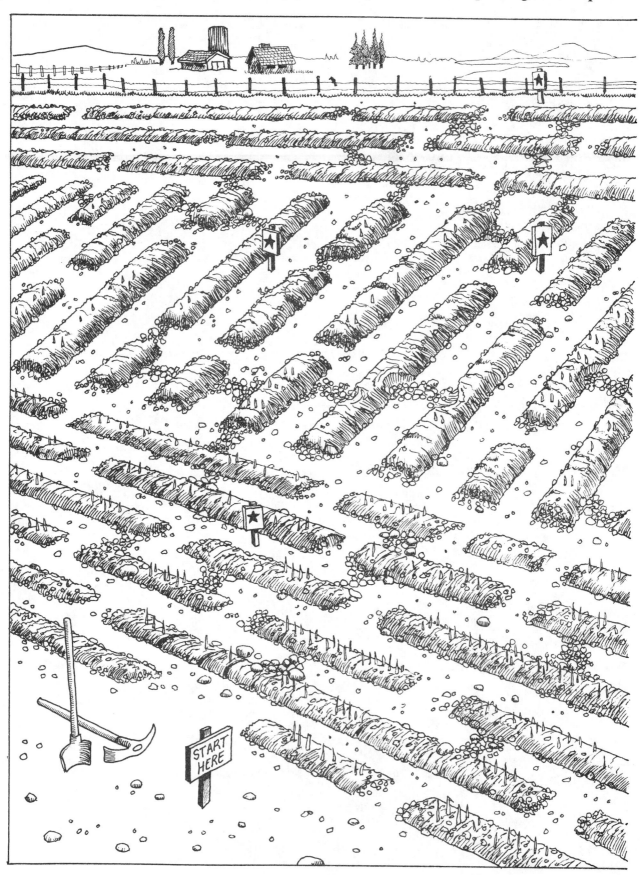

at each place he has put a star sign. Find a clear path and dig a pond at each sign. Do not backtrack. When you get to the water valve, flood the field to fill the ponds.

SAVE THE SPOTTED OWL

Save this family of spotted owls by finding a clear path to them and take them to an uncut forest.

FEED THE BABY EAGLES

Every eagle is a treasure. These babies have lost their mother. Find a clear path up the trail, climb the tree, and feed them.

SAVE THE ELEPHANTS AND RHINOS

Animals with ivory tusks are endangered and are protected from hunting. But poachers, men who hunt against the law, try to kill them to sell the ivory. Another

way to protect these animals is to cut off their ivory tusks. This does not hurt the animal, and they will not be hunted. Save the elephant and rhinos by finding a clear path to them and cut off their tusks.

ARREST THE POACHER

This mountain gorilla is in grave danger. A poacher waits in hiding. Find a clear path and arrest the poacher.

START HERE

157

SAVE THE RAIN FOREST

This rain forest is in danger of being cut down. Cutting down the rain forests

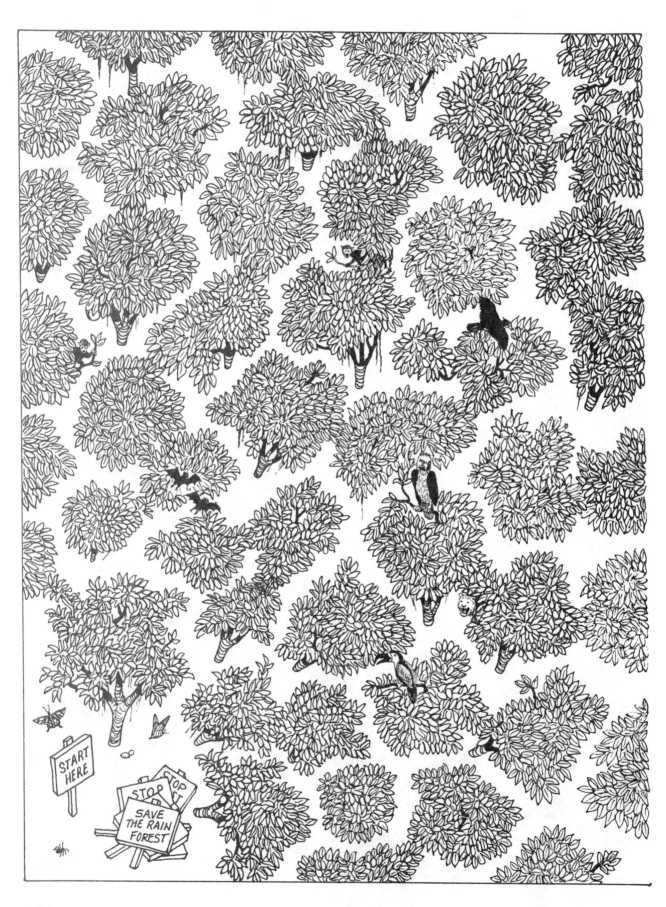

threatens life on the entire planet. Find a clear path and put these signs where the cutting crew has left their saws.

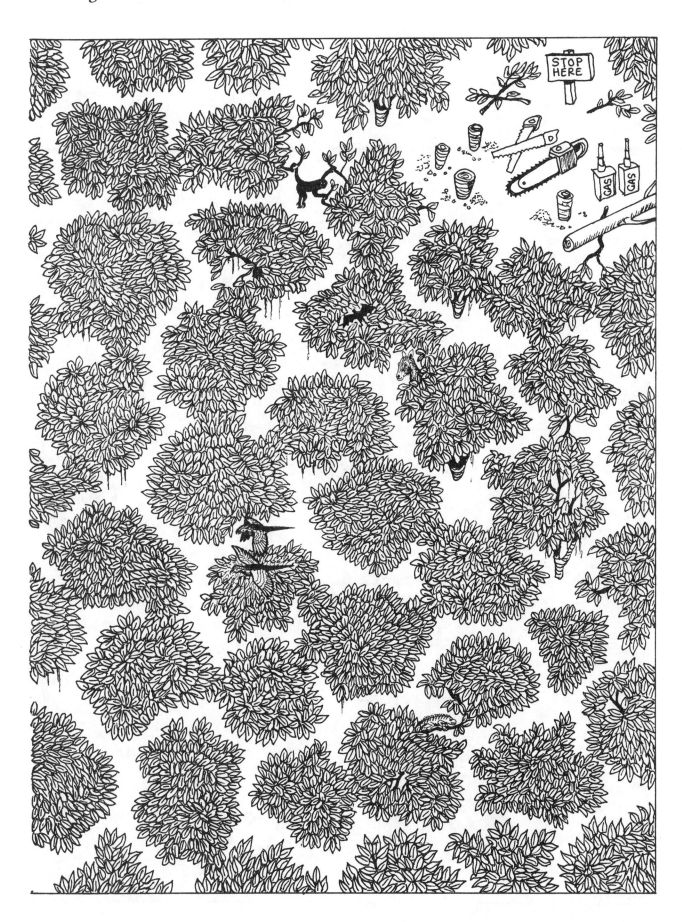

SAVE THE PANDA
Pandas are almost extinct because they are slow to get together and produce

offspring. They sometimes die off faster than they reproduce. Help this male panda find a clear path to the female in the upper right.

SAVE THE CALIFORNIA CONDOR

Only a few California condors exist, raised in captivity. Some have been released into the wild. Help them survive. Find a clear path to the cave and leave the condor food.

Pollution

Man's carelessness has polluted the earth so much that man himself is in danger. We dump and spill pollutants into the water and onto the land. Acid rain is caused by pollutants that get into the air and fall back to earth in the rain. These pollutants kill fish and wildlife. We must stop pollution and clean things up if we are to survive.

FIGHT THE OIL SPILL

This oil spill is a big mess. To save the birds and seal that are covered with oil, you must quickly find a clear path through the mess.

STOP ACID RAIN

The white bricks stick out just enough from this pollutant spewing chimney so you can climb to the top and put a filter on it. Climb only on the connecting white bricks.

START ON ANY LIGHT COLORED BRICK AT THE BASE OF THE CHIMNEY

CHIMNEY FILTER KIT

STOP NUCLEAR WASTE DUMPING

These trucks are going to dump radioactive waste into the canyon. Get up the trail in a hurry and stop them. Time is short. Hopefully, you'll be right the first time.

CLEAN UP THE PARK

The junk littering this once beautiful picnic area needs to be hauled away, but the removal truck is broken down. Find a clear path through the field and fix the truck.

STOP LAKE POLLUTION

This pipe is leaking toxic, industrial waste. Put the cork in it to stop the pollution of

this freshwater lake. As you row, find your way through clean white water. Do not get any pollution on you or the boat.

PRODUCE FRESH DRINKING WATER

Place clean ice blocks from the high mountains into the funnel and find your way down the pipes to open the valve and fill the bottles. It is OK to go behind other pipes.

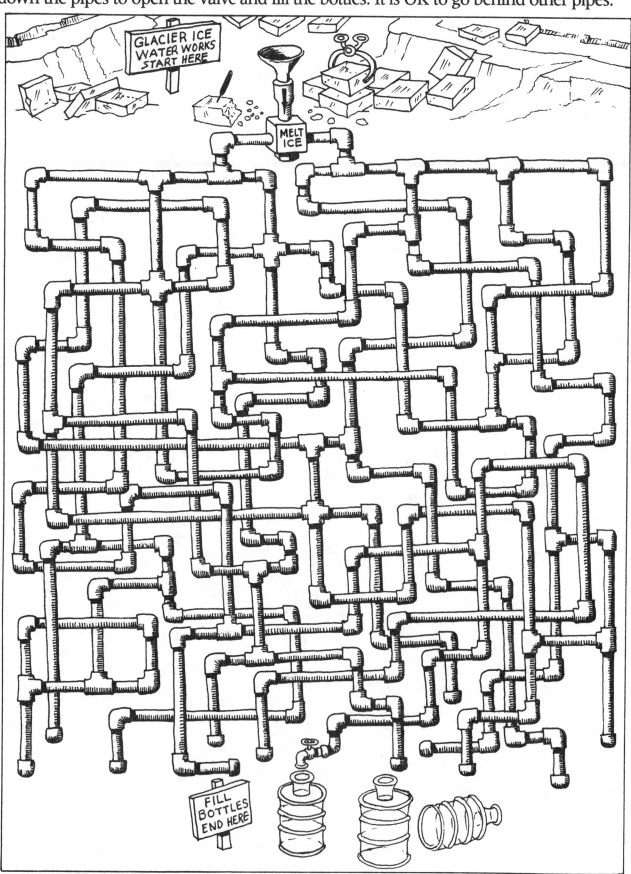

STOP AIR POLLUTION

A van on this freeway is polluting the air. Take the patrol car and arrest the driver. Be careful you don't get off on the wrong freeway.

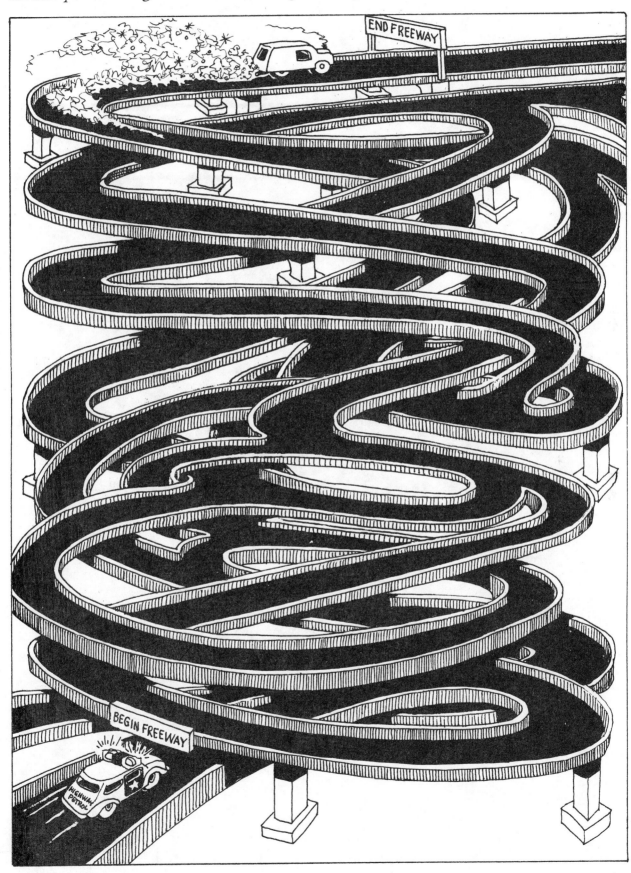

Congratulations!

Mother Earth thanks you for a job well done. You have come to understand that she is fragile and that her problems are very serious. More than two billion people throughout the world lack safe drinking water. Increased carbon dioxide, methane, and other gases in our atmosphere could have disastrous consequences. Scientists have estimated that 1.2 million species of animals will vanish during the next quarter century. It is a fact that it will take a worldwide collective effort to reverse such conditions if we are to save the Earth.

Some people have already started. Large-scale efforts have shown that soil erosion and land destruction can be stopped when a real effort is made. Tropical forests do not have to be leveled in order to feed people.

We have all the resources we need to start bringing our world into balance with nature. Many countries have been increasing their efforts to recycle waste, eliminate air pollution, and manage natural resources. The situation is not hopeless.

To save the Earth, it takes people who have courage, strength, self-motivation, and a desire to be part of the solution—not part of the problem. You have demonstrated, through your efforts in this book, that you have these characteristics and concerns. As you work to rebuild the world, know that the time has come. Be a leader and encourage others to follow your example.

Good luck.

Help for Earth Savers

The world's problems are difficult. It is not unlikely that you could have run into some problems along the way. If you need help or want to check how you did, the keys to the mazes follow.

Save the Dolphin

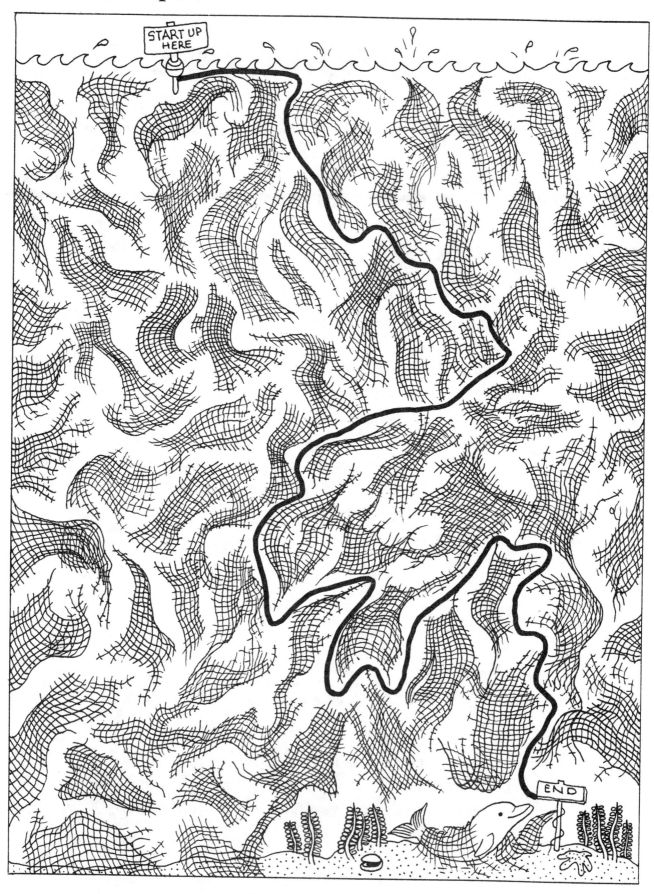

Free the Fishes

START HERE

END HERE

START HERE

ENTER OCEAN UNDER BRIDGE

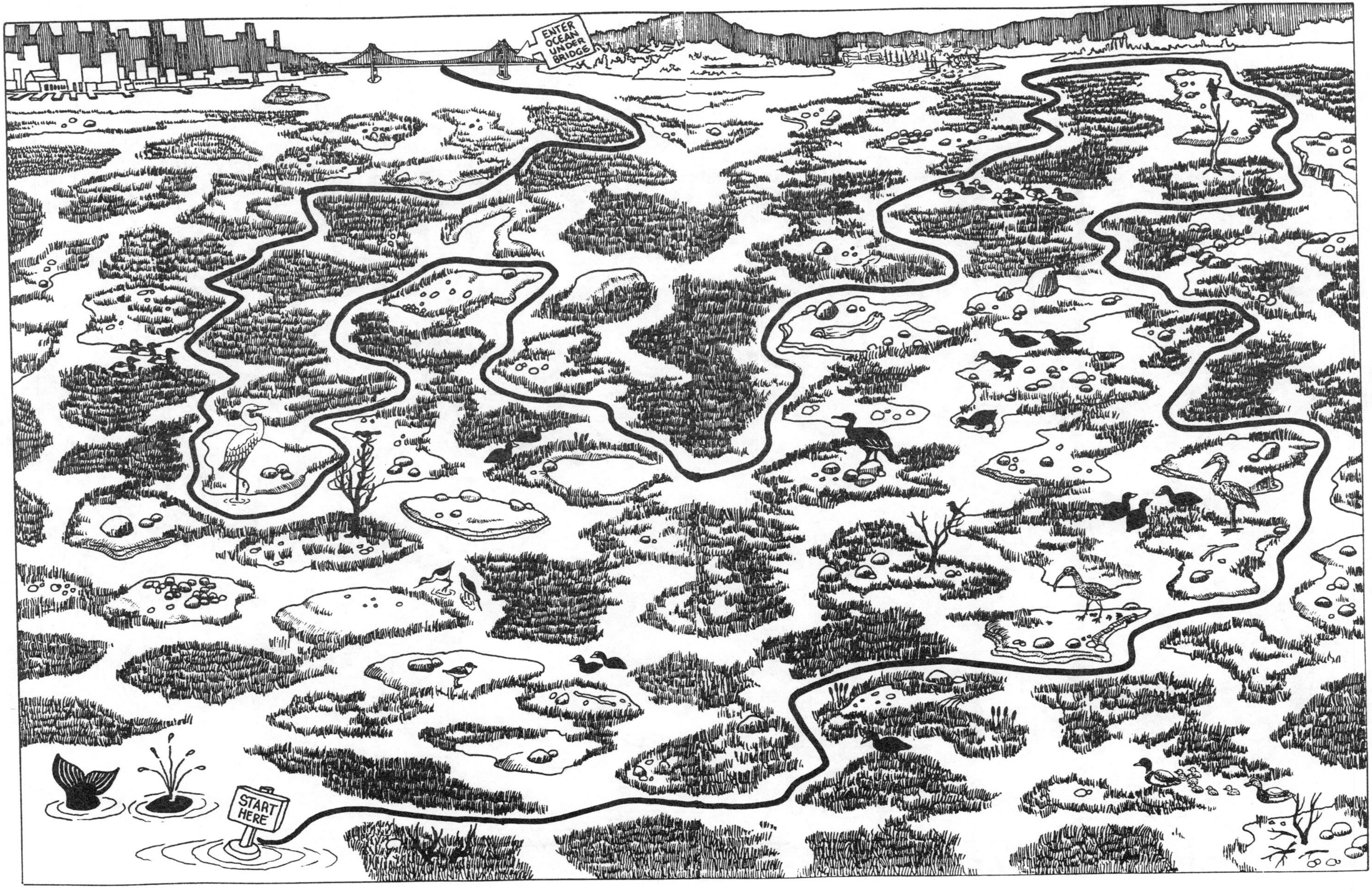

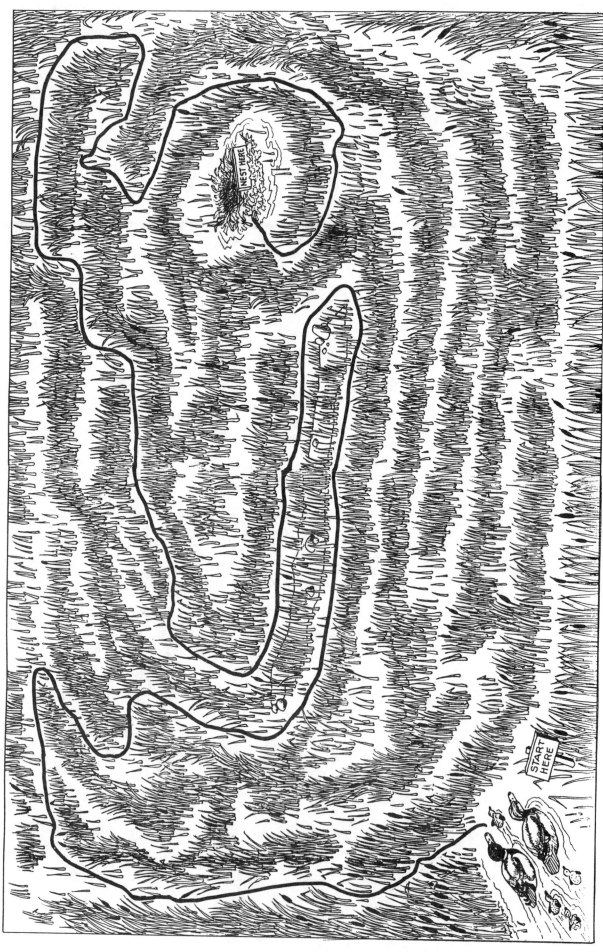

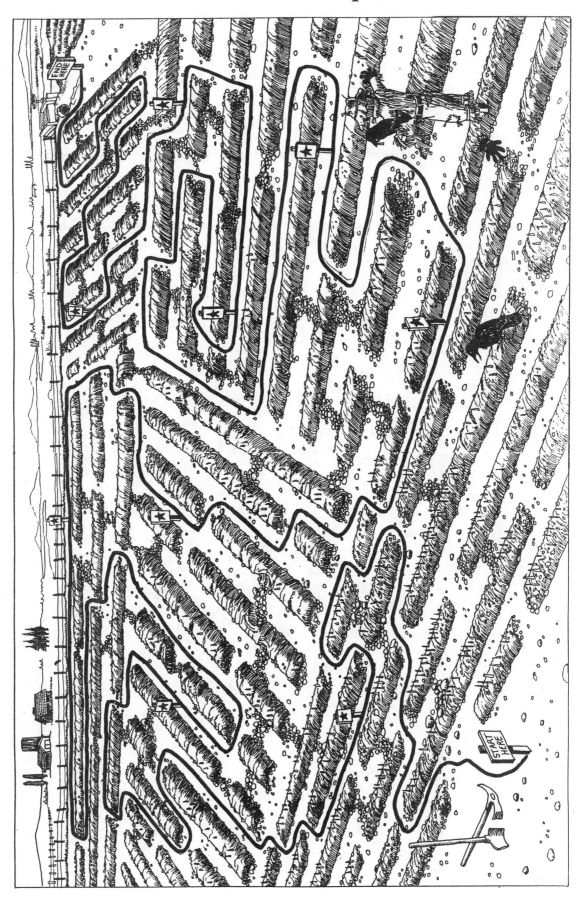

Save the Spotted Owl

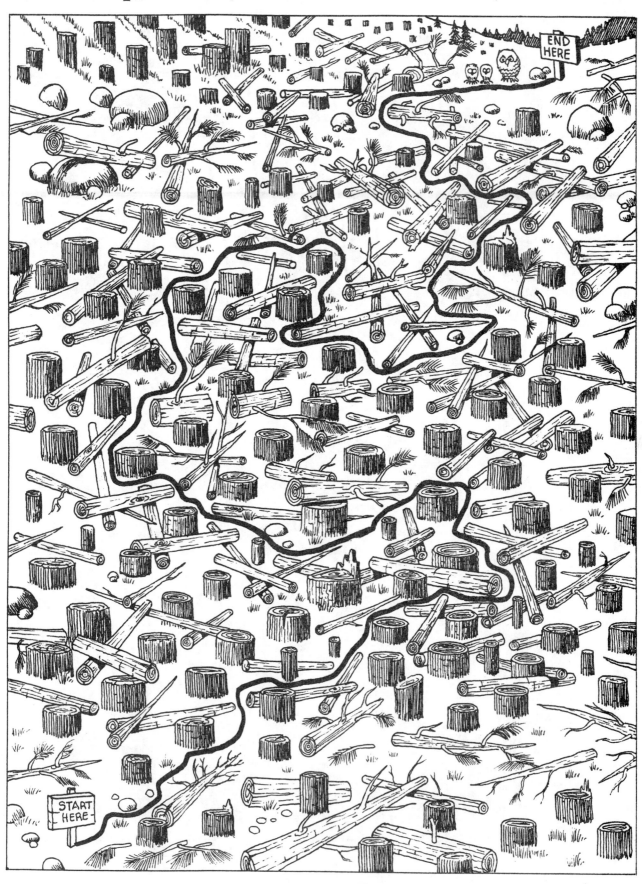

184

Arrest the Poacher

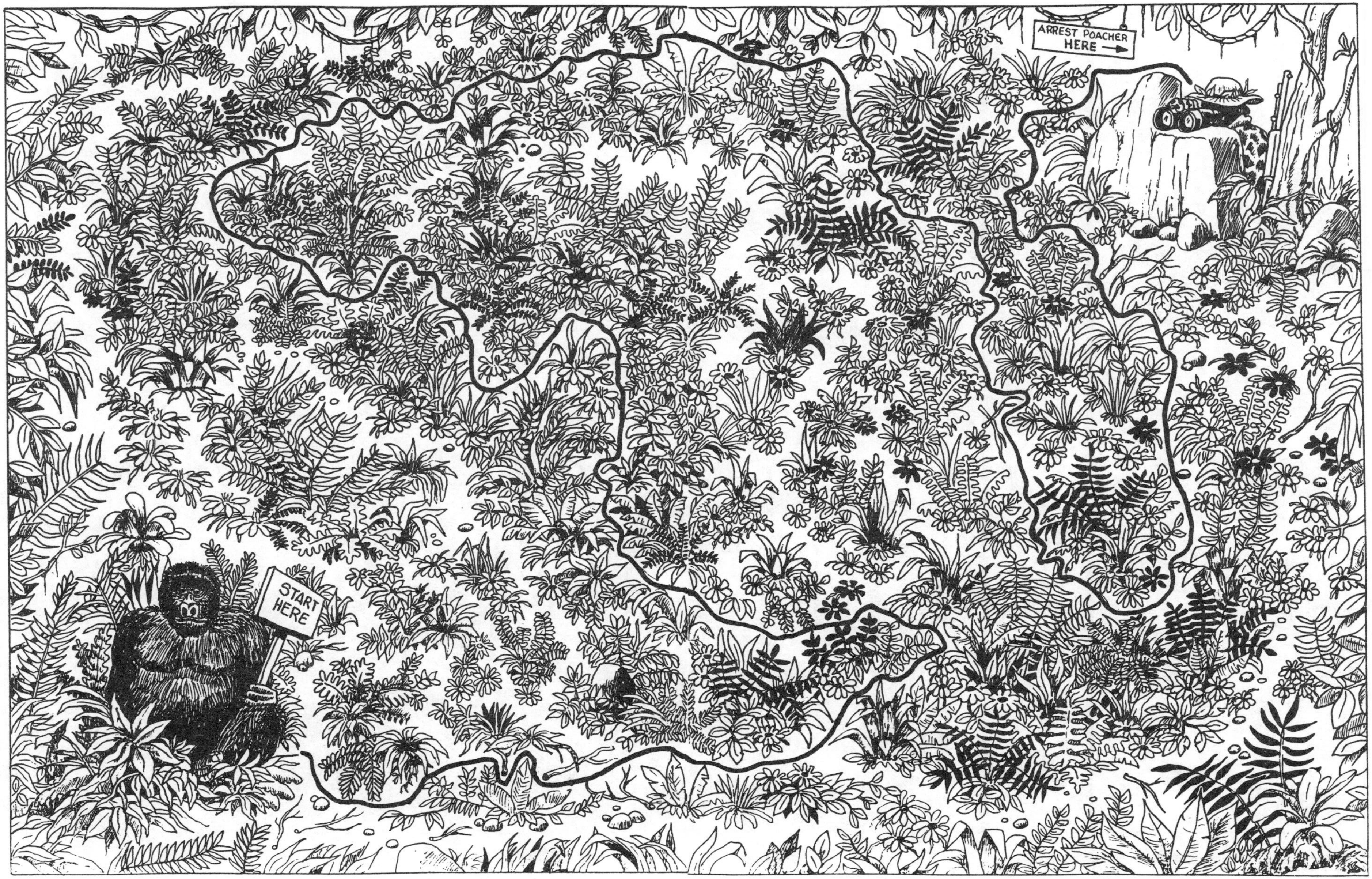

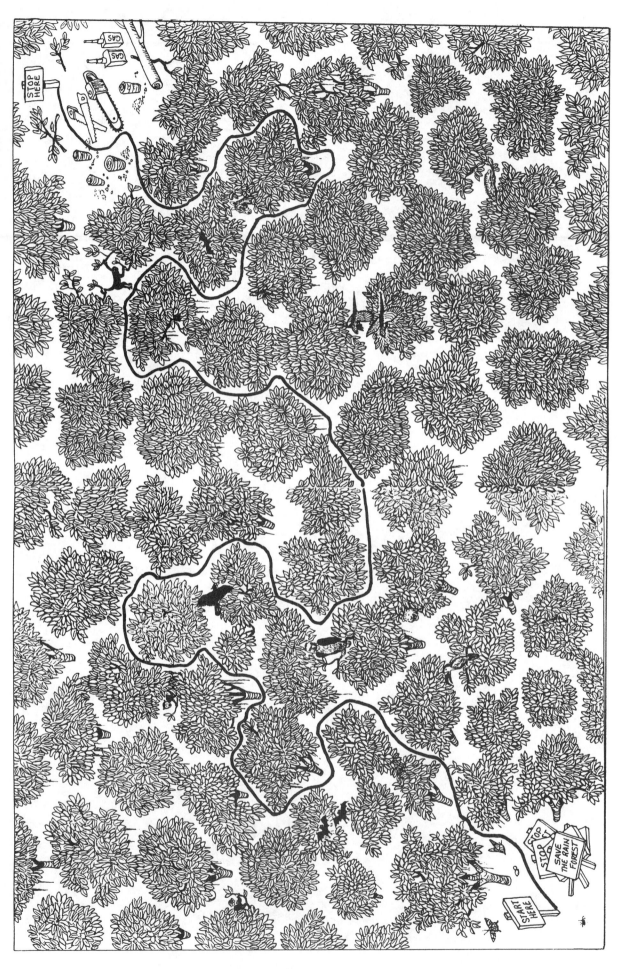

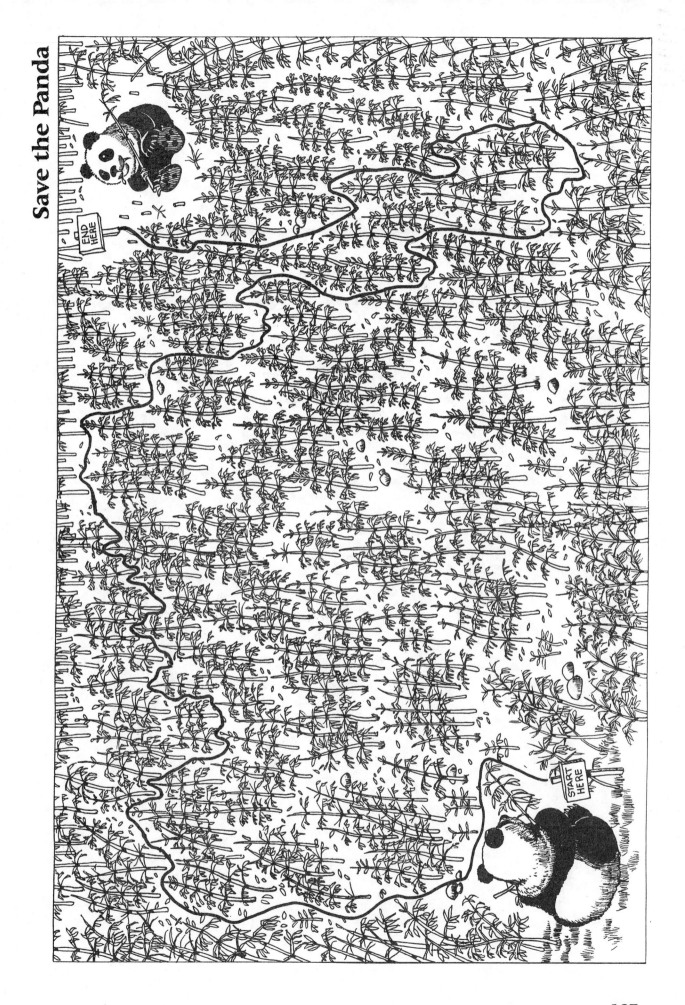

Save the California Condor

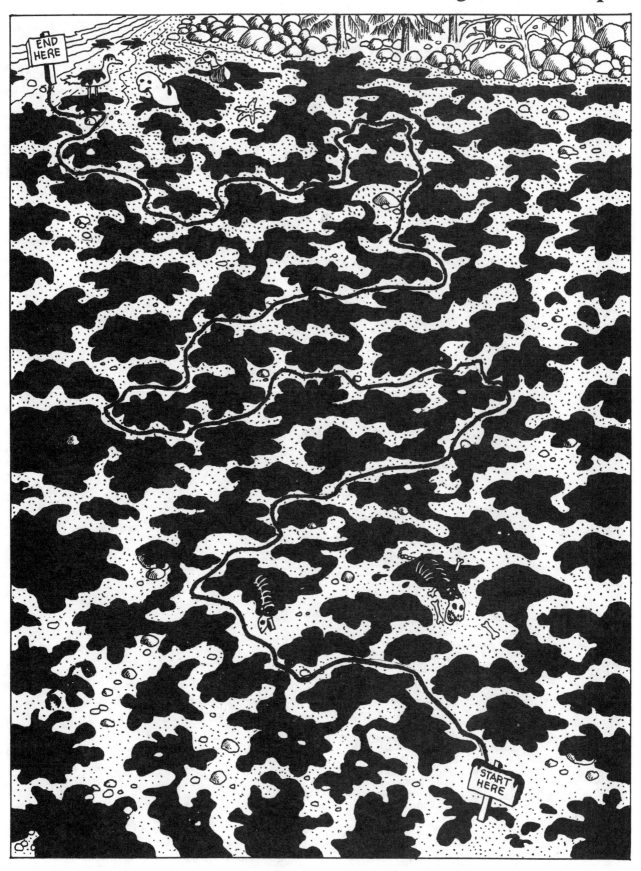

Stop Acid Rain

Clean Up the Park

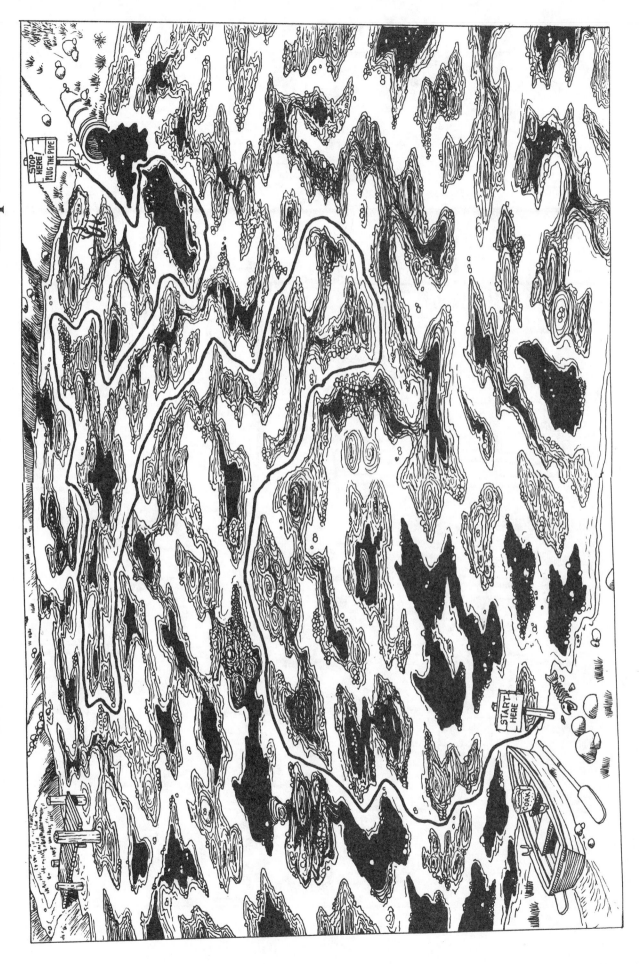

Produce Fresh Drinking Water

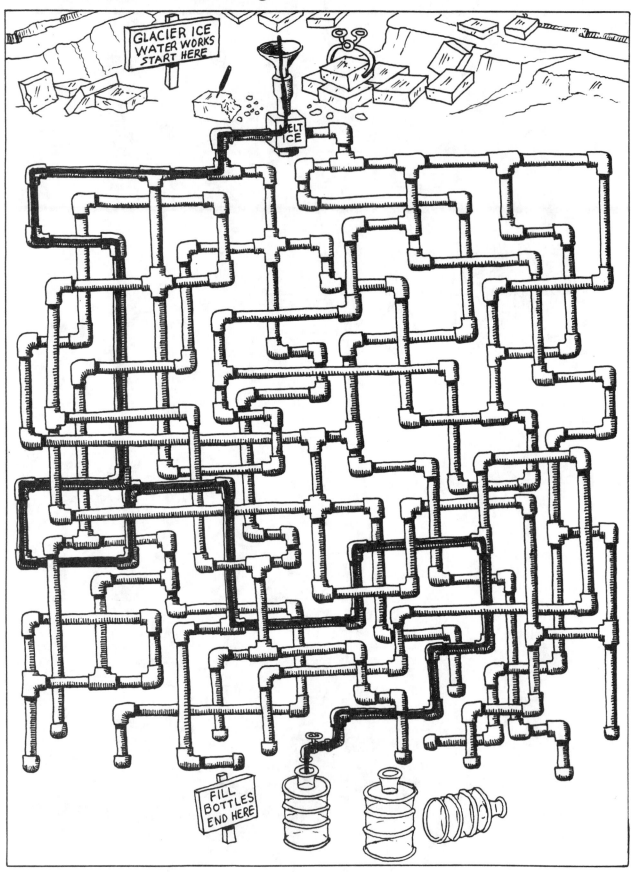

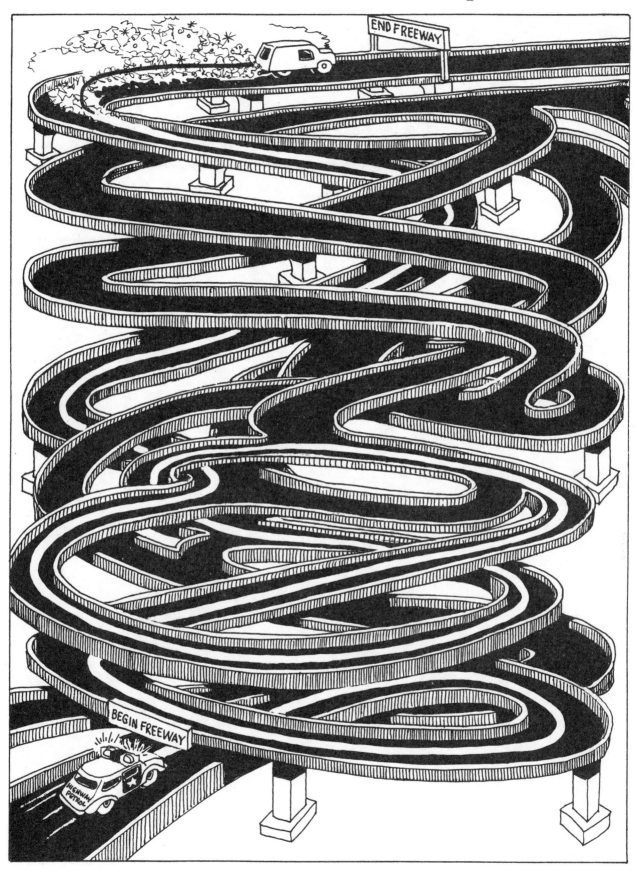

MOUNTAIN MAZES

Contents

INTRODUCTION

Climbing to the top of a high mountain is challenging, but also exhilarating and rewarding. During the second half of the twentieth century, mountain climbing has become increasingly popular. In 1953, when the British made the first ascent of Mount Everest, the highest mountain in the world, the age of mountaineering came alive. Most of the highest peaks in the world have been climbed since then. Increased emphasis on physical fitness, improved equipment and modernized modes of travel have made such quests more feasible.

In 1981, two Americans, Frank Wells and Dick Bass, set the ambitious goal of being the first to climb to the top of the highest mountain on each of the seven continents. Although these mountains had been previously conquered, no one had attempted to subdue all of the "seven summits." It was a daunting task, but in 1985, Dick Bass became the first to complete the ascent of all seven summits.

Time and expense prevent most mountaineers from journeying to each of the seven continents and climbing its highest mountain. But regardless of what factors might keep you from having such an adventure, you can climb the seven summits right here, right now. Before you go, however, you must learn the techniques of climbing and get into shape by doing the climbs on the next few pages. Learn ice climbing by climbing the Nisqually Glacier on Mount Rainier in Washington. When climbing Rainier, stay on the trail and avoid falling into the crevasses. Find a clear trail to the summit. Next, learn to rock-climb by climbing the face of El Capitan in Yosemite, California. Climb the ropes by finding a continual rope link to the summit. In some places you may have to descend a rope in order to find your way to the top. Finally, get into shape by climbing the highest mountain in the contiguous United States, 14,497-foot Mount Whitney in the High Sierras of California. Find a clear path and climb the ropes until you can reach the summit. You cannot step over any rocks and you may have to descend ropes in order to find your way.

When these practice climbs are complete, you will be ready to begin your journey to climb the seven summits. You will have to make many difficult and important decisions along the way. Just remember you will be successful if you don't give up. Good luck.

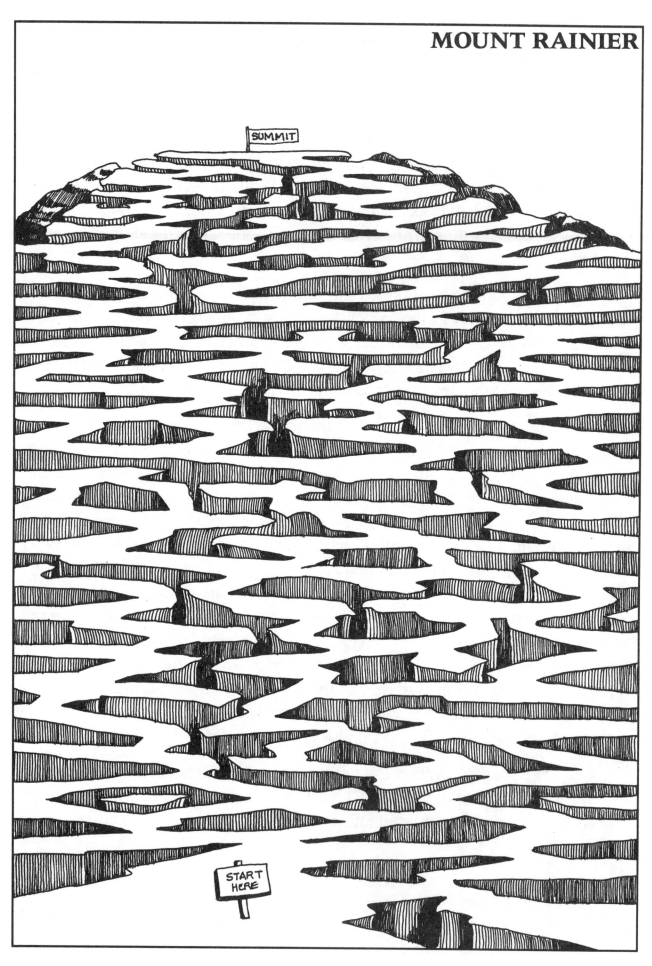

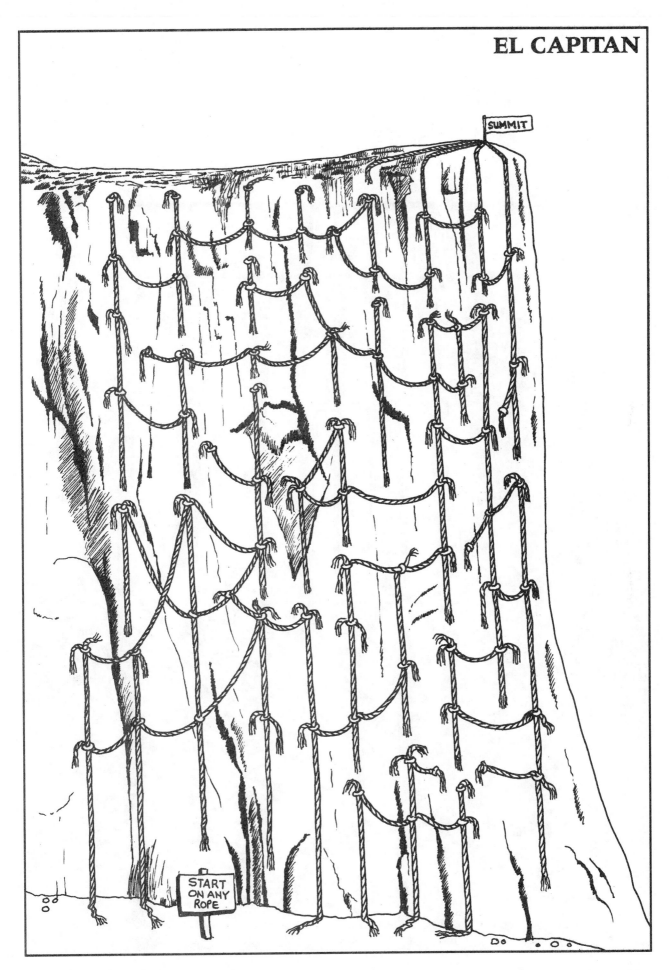

SUMMIT

START ON ANY ROPE

START HERE

SUMMIT

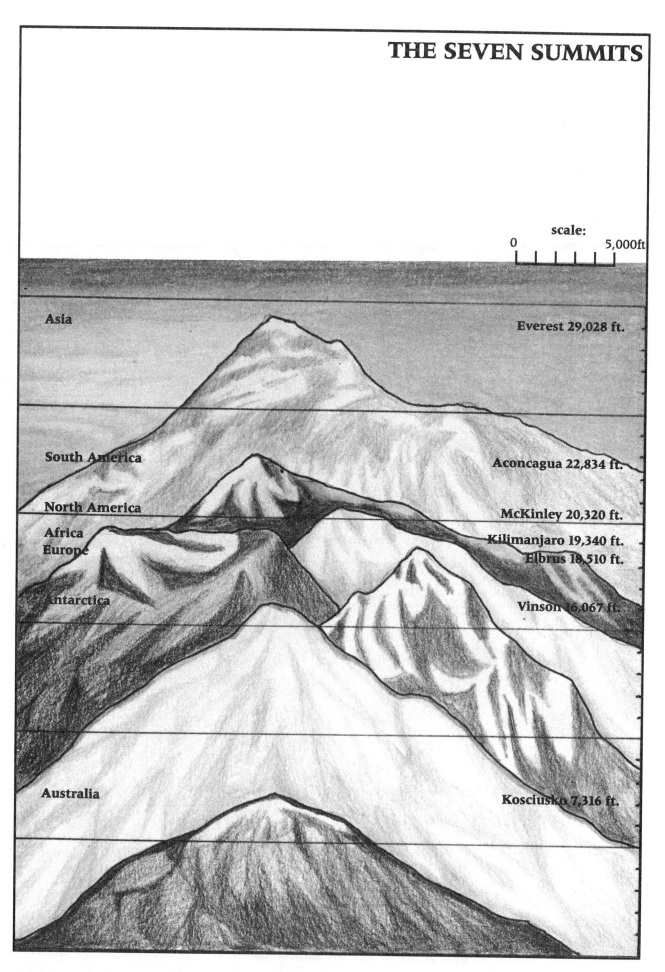

THE SEVEN SUMMITS

scale:

0   5,000ft

Asia   Everest 29,028 ft.

South America   Aconcagua 22,834 ft.

North America   McKinley 20,320 ft.

Africa   Kilimanjaro 19,340 ft.

Europe   Elbrus 18,510 ft.

Antarctica   Vinson 16,067 ft.

Australia   Kosciusko 7,316 ft.

AUSTRALIA

Australia is the smallest continent and the only continent that is a country. Because it lies entirely south of the equator, Australia is sometimes called the Land Down Under. It is low and flat except for mountains along the eastern coast and a few high areas in the interior. The highest mountain in Australia is Mount Kosciusko.

Kosciusko
7,316 ft.

MOUNT KOSCIUSKO
7,316 FEET

Mount Kosciusko is in the Muniong range of the Australian Alps in southeastern New South Wales. At 7,316 feet, this mountain is the lowest of the seven summits. Because of its height and mild terrain, it is not considered a difficult mountain to climb. Who made the first ascent is unknown. Likely the summit was reached centuries ago by some tribesmen seeking a high-vantage viewpoint.

Begin your climb at the bottom left corner. Your challenge is to find a clear pathway between the rocks to the summit. Do not step over any rocks. Take your time and have a nice hike.

Special note: Some geographers include the islands near Australia as part of the Australian continent—namely Oceania or Australasia. Included would be the island of New Guinea. The highest peak of Australasia is 16,023 foot Carstensz Pyramid on New Guinea. It was first climbed in 1936. If you prefer to climb Carstensz Pyramid rather than Kosciusko, you can make that substitution.

START HERE

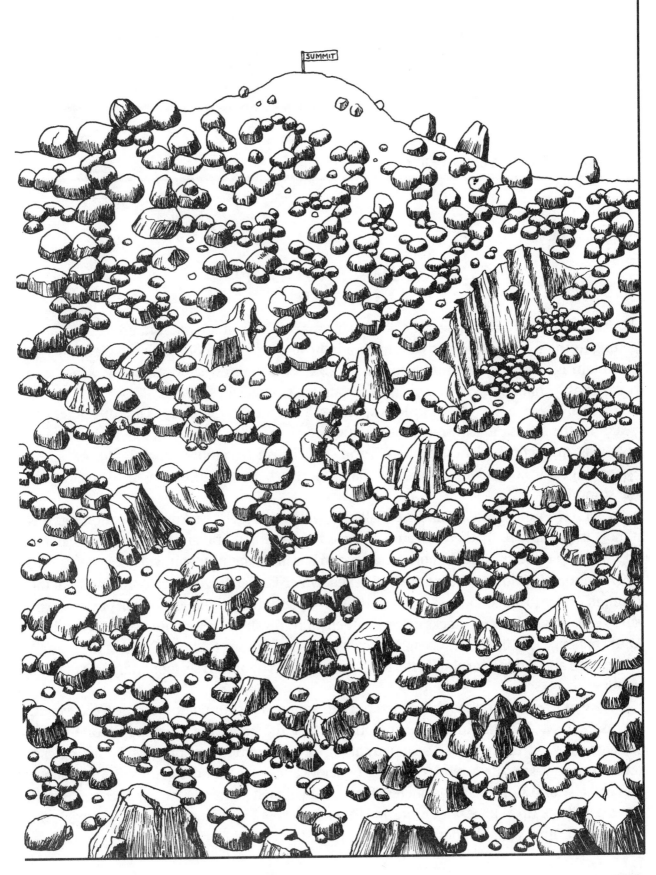

ANTARCTICA

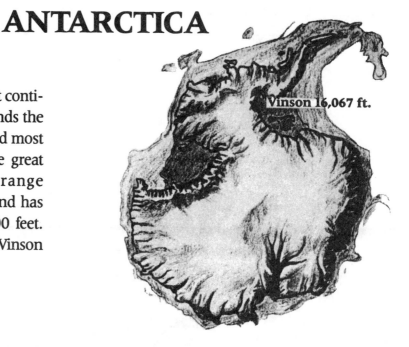

Vinson 16,067 ft.

Antarctica is the fifth-largest continent in the world and surrounds the South Pole. It is the coldest and most desolate region on earth. The great Transantarctic mountain range crosses the entire continent and has peaks rising as high as 16,000 feet. The highest of these is Mount Vinson at 16,067 feet.

MOUNT VINSON
16,067 FEET

Mount Vinson's location near the South Pole makes this a unique mountain to climb. Just getting to the mountain in such a remote and hostile environment creates challenges. This mountain is always covered with ice and snow. Temperatures below zero, icy winds and occasional "whiteouts" keep climbers in a constant struggle for survival.

In 1966, however, an American-led expedition set out to climb many of the unchallenged peaks in the Transantarctic range. They succeeded in climbing many, but their ultimate goal was Antarctica's highest peak—Vinson. Finally, on December 18, at 11:30 A.M., Pete Schoening, Bill Long, John Evans and Barry Corbet became the first men to set foot on the summit.

To get to Mount Vinson, your first challenge will be to reach the Antarctic continent. It is almost impossible to fly there because of the difficulty in landing and taking off on ice and snow. Going by ship is much more feasible, and it will be the way you will go.

The mountain is located near the Weddell Sea, which is often frozen over for miles. Breaking through the ice to reach shore can only be done by a special ship designed for that purpose. The ship's captain will look for cracks in the ice, then guide his ship through until shore is reached. Your challenge is to find a clear passage through the Weddell Sea to shore. Begin at the bottom of the page and guide your ship to the top. There you will be able to set foot onto the Antarctic continent.

Now you're ready to climb the second peak in your seven-summit quest—the ice-covered, crevasse-strewn Mount Vinson. Begin your climb at the bottom of the page on one of the snowy pathways. You must find a safe way along the path without stepping over or falling into any of the crevasses. Be careful. Climbing on snow and ice is very dangerous. Snow bridges can collapse and slopes can avalanche. If you find yourself going the wrong direction, don't hesitate to back up, retrace your route and find a new way. Your determination not to give up will pay off. Trust your abilities. You will reach the top.

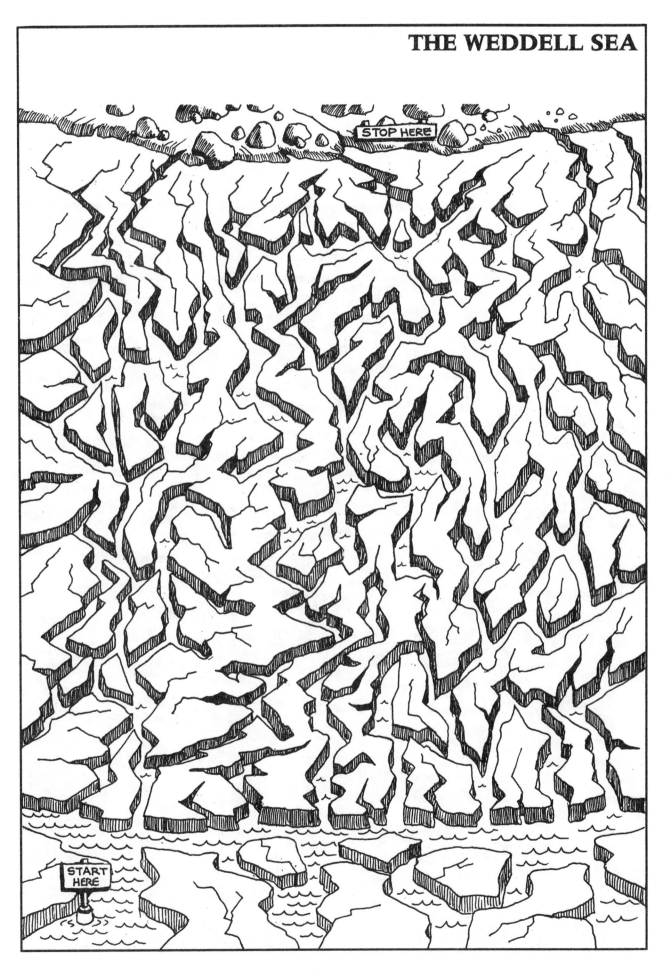

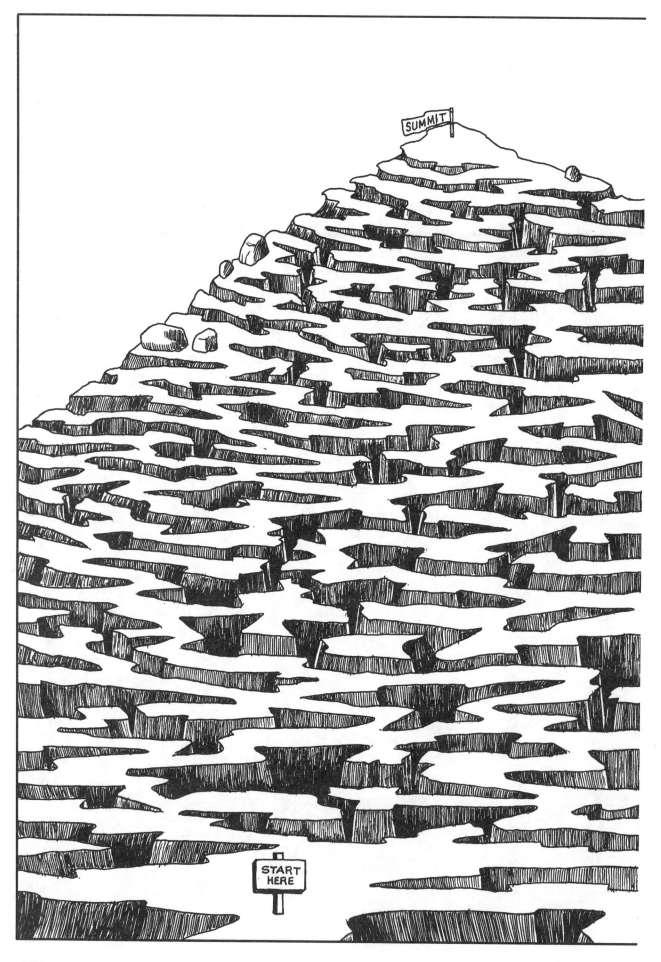

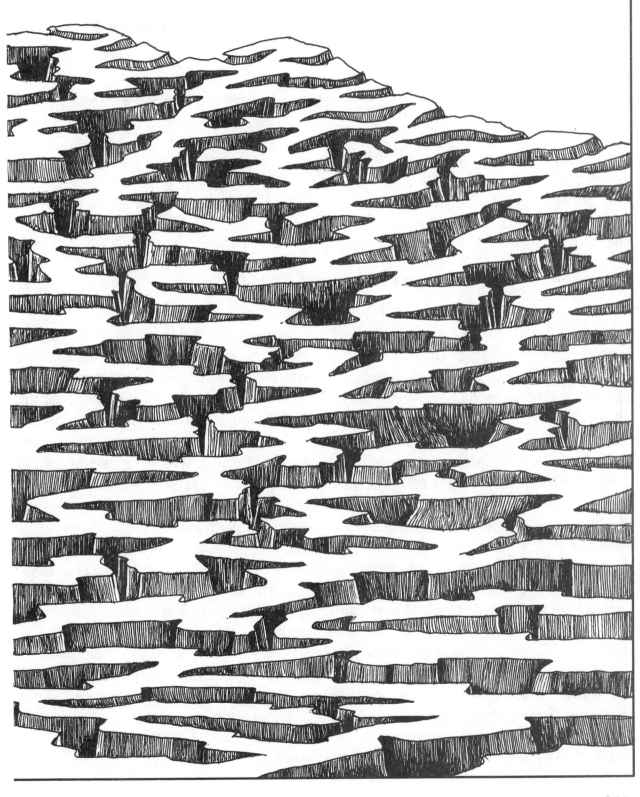

EUROPE

Europe is one of the smallest continents—only Australia is smaller. Yet it has a larger population than all of the other continents except Asia.

A series of Alpine mountain ranges traverses southern Europe. From west to east, this includes the Sierra Nevada, the Pyrenees, the Alps, the Apennines, the Carpathians, the Balkans and the Caucasus. Mount Elbrus, at 18,510 feet, is the highest mountain in Europe and is in the Caucasus.

Elbrus 18,510 ft.

MOUNT ELBRUS
18,510 FEET

Mount Elbrus is an extinct volcano. It was first climbed in 1868 by Douglas W. Freshfield. Because of its height, it is covered with snow and a number of glaciers descend from its summit. Technically, it is not considered a difficult mountain to climb. However, its high altitude can cause problems, especially if a climber ascends too fast. Oxygen gets thinner the higher the altitude, so it is important to climb slowly and to gradually acclimatize to the altitude. Otherwise, altitude sickness is a real threat—headache, nausea, lack of appetite and poor or no sleep. Freshfield experienced this during his historic first ascent of the mountain.

To get to Mount Elbrus, you must hike up the trail to the plateau at the foot of the mountain. Over the years, rocks falling from the mountain have littered the path that crosses the plateau, blocking the way. Over the years, climbers have made new paths around the rocks, but rocks continue to fall. Now there are many paths that cannot be used. Fortunately, a recent expedition cleared a path for you. You must find that path. It will not be blocked by rocks. Begin your approach from the left. Exit on the right. The mountain will be straight ahead.

Now you are ready to climb Mount Elbrus. Go slowly. This will help prevent mountain sickness. Look around carefully. This will minimize the risk of getting lost. Start your climb at the bottom left corner of the page. Your challenge is to find a clear pathway to the mountain's summit. Be careful to avoid the crevasses as you get higher on the mountain. Don't hesitate to descend and to set out in a new direction if you get off the right route. Remember, you cannot step over the rocks that are in your way; and you cannot jump over crevasses.

The conquest of Elbrus will be your third victory. You will have four to go. There are some tough climbs ahead, but if anyone can succeed, you can. Be tough!

START
HERE

AFRICA

Africa is the second-largest continent in the world. It is a land of varied, scenic beauty best described in superlatives. It has the largest desert, the longest river, the longest freshwater lake, and some of the most spectacular waterfalls. The highest mountain is Kilimanjaro in Tanzania. Although it is near the equator, ice and snow cover much of it all year round.

Kilimanjaro 19,340 ft.

MOUNT KILIMANJARO
19,340 FEET

Mount Kilimanjaro is a volcano with smoke still rising from its huge summit crater. It dominates the horizon as its bulk rises out of the Tanzanian lowlands. Hans Meyer and his guide, Ludwig Partscheller, were the first to reach the summit in 1889. They had no trouble keeping the mountain in view as they trekked overland to reach the mountain base. But they did have trouble with the tropical heat and the distance they had to travel. If it hadn't been for the mountain's visibility, they possibly would have given up or become lost. The only problem they had on the actual climb was the altitude, as Kilimanjaro is almost one thousand feet higher than Mount Elbrus.

You must cross the hot Tanzanian jungle to get to the base of Kilimanjaro. Begin your trek anywhere along the dirt road on the left side of the page and trek across the page to the sign. Nothing should block your way. You must find a completely clear path. Tree branches cannot block your path, and you can only cross rivers by crossing bridges. When you reach the sign, turn the page and you can begin your climb of the volcano. Again, a clear path must be found. Do not step over rocks. Your goal is the highest point on the right side of the summit.

START
ANYWHERE
ALONG THIS
ROAD.

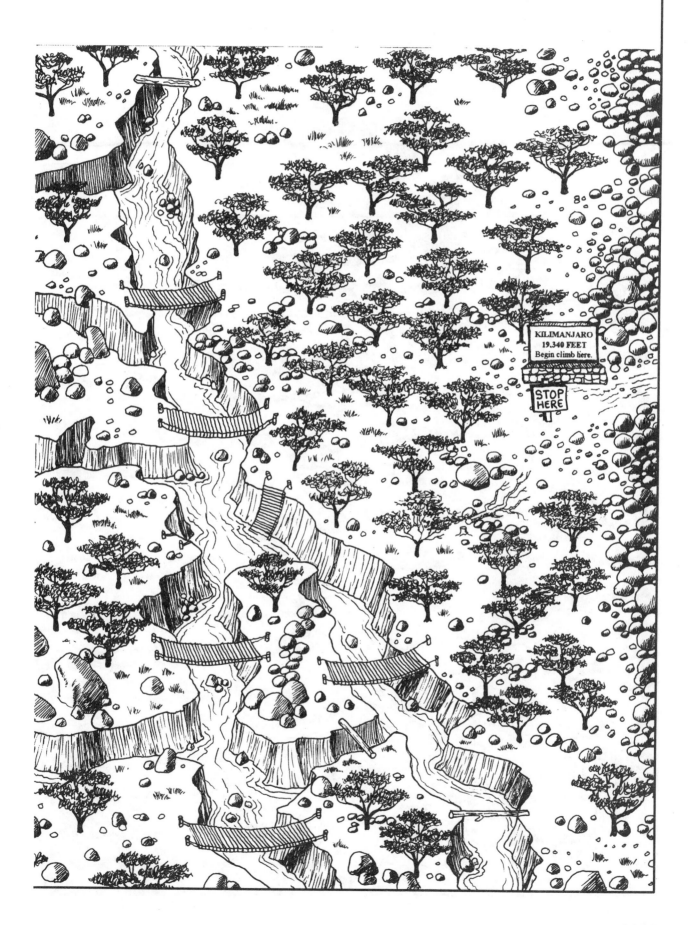

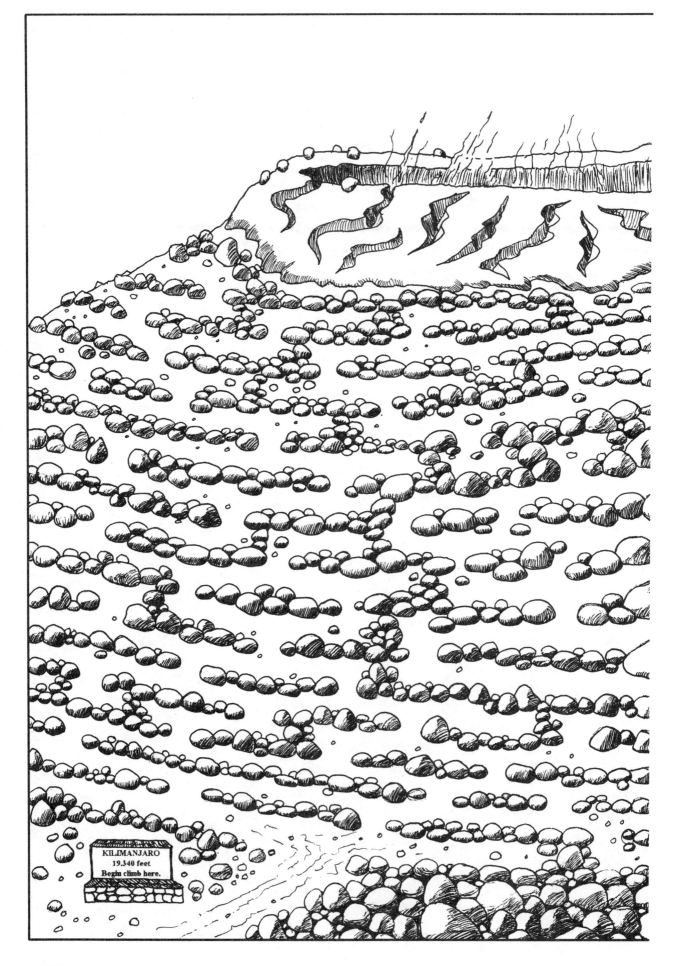

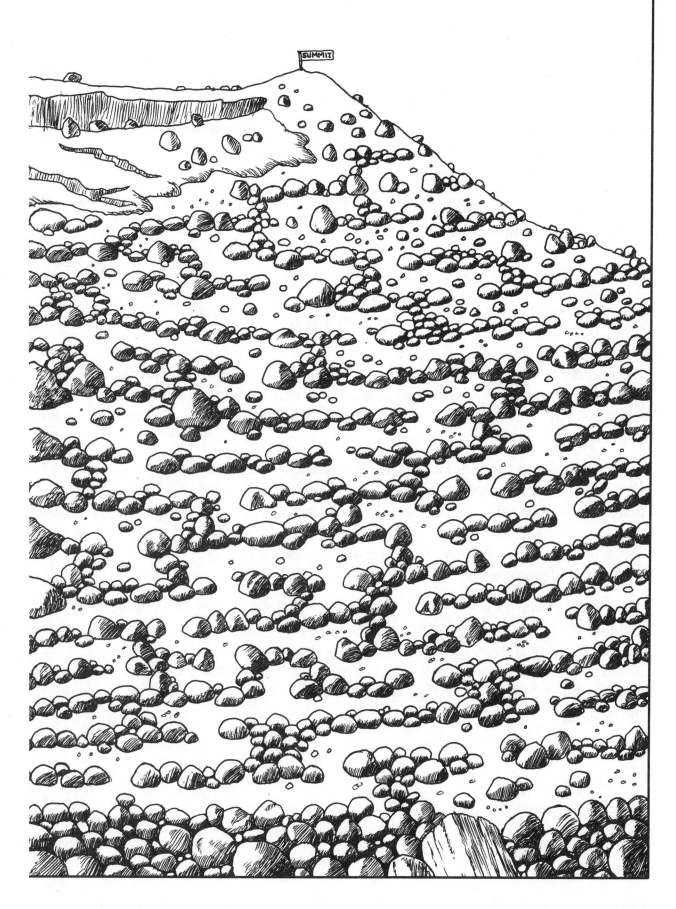

NORTH AMERICA

North America is the third-largest of the seven continents. It juts into the frigid Arctic Ocean to the north and languishes lazily in warm tropic breezes to the south. The Pacific Ocean laps along its western side and the Atlantic Ocean washes against it down its eastern side. Mount McKinley is the highest peak on the North American continent.

McKinley
20,320 ft.

MOUNT MC KINLEY
20,320 FEET

Mount McKinley is in the state of Alaska. This mountain offers danger and difficulty. Being so far north, almost within the Arctic Circle, altitude is only one consideration when climbing this mountain. Planning has to include the eventuality of extremely cold temperatures and unpredictable weather.

In 1913, Archdeacon Hudson Stuck, Harry P. Karstens and two companions were the first to climb to McKinley's summit. Many have since summited this mountain. Climbers once had to trek for weeks to reach McKinley's base. Today, within a few hours, they can be dropped off by airplane at the foot of the mountain's glaciers. The actual climb begins by ascending these dangerous glaciers until the base of the mountain itself is reached, and then up the snowy slopes and ridges to the top.

On climbs over great snowfields, where the weather can turn bad quickly and cause "whiteouts," climbers put up marker poles linked with ropes so they can find their way up and down. On the next page, the marker poles and ropes are in place. Some of the ropes have broken, but the correct route to the top is marked with an unbroken rope link from pole to pole. Start at the bottom. You must find the correct route by climbing the unbroken rope line to the summit.

THE GLACIERS

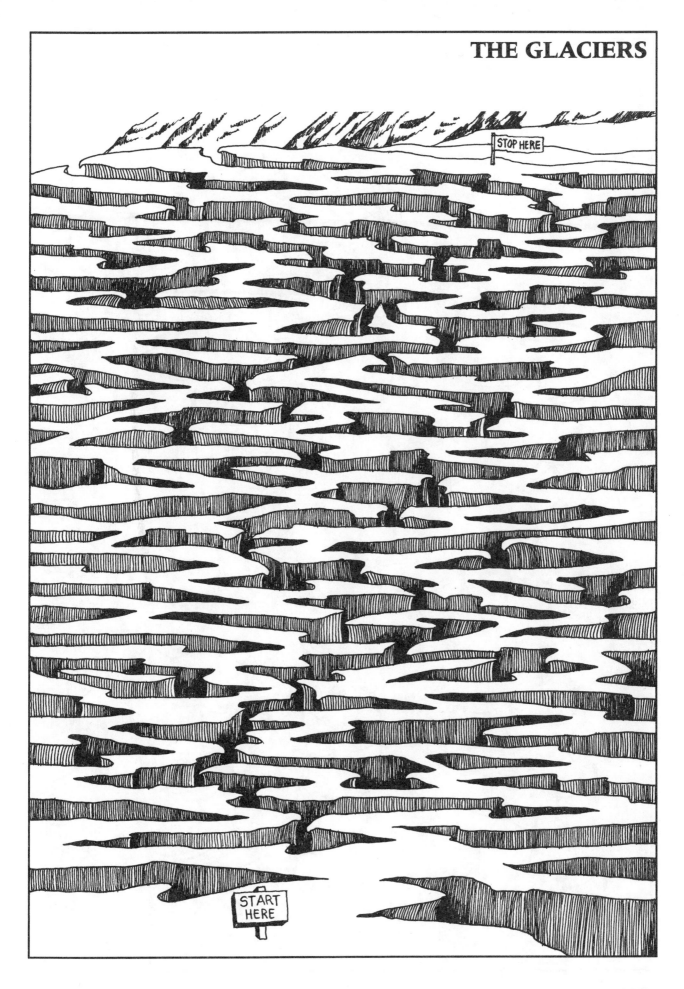

225

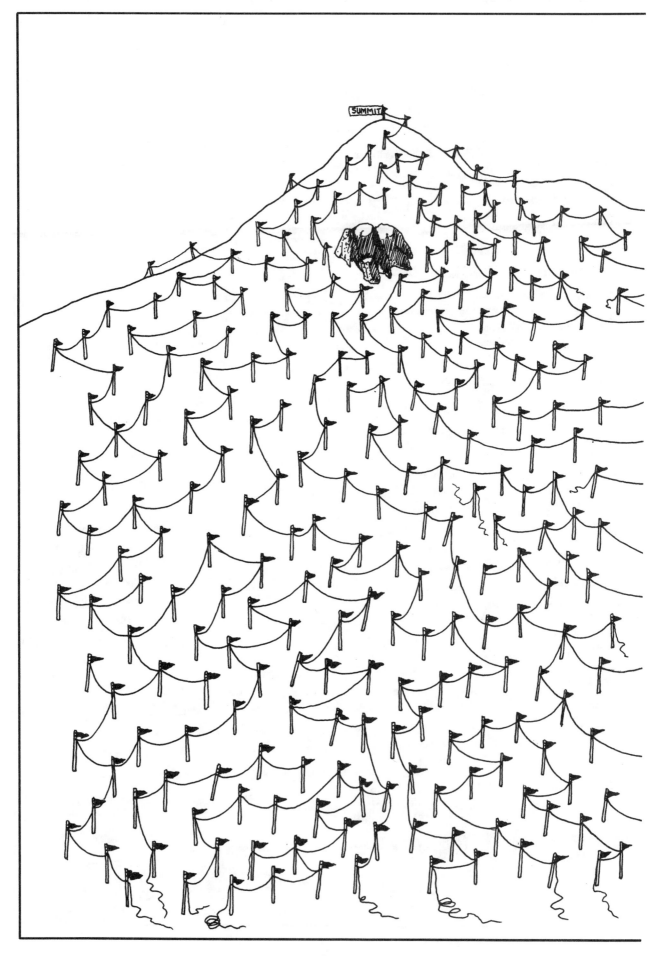

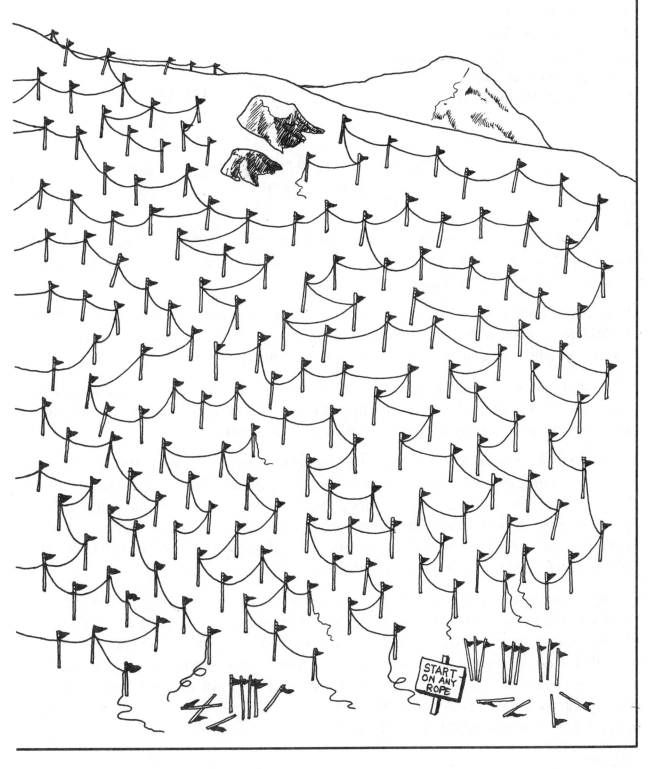

START ON ANY ROPE

SOUTH AMERICA

South America is the fourth-largest continent. North America trails down into the northern border of South America and South America continues south to within 600 miles of Antarctica. The equator extends across the continent at almost its widest point. The great Andes Mountains extend along the entire western coast of South America.

Aconcagua 22,834 ft.

MOUNT ACONCAGUA
22,834 FEET

In the Andean mountain range of South America, more than fifty peaks rise to over 20,000 feet. Aconcagua, at 22,834 feet, is the highest peak on this continent. It is located in Argentina where the Andes brush its western edge.

Shortly before the turn of the century, a British expedition, under the leadership of Edward A. Fitzgerald, made several attempts to be the first to climb the mountain. It was Matthew Zurbriggen who arrived alone on the lofty summit January 14, 1897.

Snow and ice continually cover Aconcagua's upper slopes, but it is the high altitude that makes this peak a tough challenge. It is more than 2,500 feet higher than Mount McKinley, making Aconcagua the highest peak in the Western Hemisphere.

Getting to Aconcagua requires miles of hiking up canyons and crossing streams. It can be very dangerous and rough going. Your task is to cross the Vacas River without falling into it. Begin your crossing of the Vacas on the left side of the canyon and cross on the bridges and logs until you reach the right side of the canyon. Be careful as you go, because many bridges and logs have collapsed. If you get off-route, back up and find a new one. When you get to the other side, you will be ready to climb the mountain.

Begin your climb at the base of the mountain. Many fixed ropes are in place from previous climbs, but some ropes have broken. You must find a continual rope link that will take you to the top. You can traverse and descend if necessary to reach the top, but you cannot move onto a rope that is not connected to the one you are on. When you reach the top, you will have conquered your sixth summit. Only the mighty Mount Everest will remain for you to climb—the highest mountain in the world. It is over 6,000 feet higher than Aconcagua. But don't despair. The skills you are gaining will enable you to conquer Everest.

ASIA

Asia is the largest of the seven continents and covers nearly one-third of the world's land area. The Himalayan mountain range is the highest in the world and is located in Asia. The highest town in the world, at 15,000 feet, is in the Himalayas. The base of the Himalayas is higher than the mountains of most countries. The highest mountain is Mount Everest, which is the most coveted climb in the world for mountaineers.

MOUNT EVEREST
29,028 FEET

Mountain Everest is an awesome mountain, not only to behold, but to climb. The Tibetans call it Chomolungma, which means goddess mother of the world. And to the Nepalese it is known as Sagarmatha, meaning sky head. For years, people tried unsuccessfully to climb Everest. As always, but to a greater degree, there were the challenges of extreme altitude, violent weather and treacherous terrain. Eventually, however, even this magnificant mountain's summit was reached. Two members of a British expedition, Edmund Hillary and a Sherpa, Tenzing Norkay, summited on May 29, 1953. Their route was on the southwestern side of the mountain. To climb Everest from this side, there are four main parts: the Khumbu glacier, the Icefall, the Lhotse face, and the south-east ridge that leads to the summit.

Now *you* must climb these four parts on the south-west route. As you approach Mount Everest, you will come to the Khumbu glacier. It is a mass of ice and snow that is covered with rocks that have fallen from the sides of Everest. You must find a way up the glacier to the Icefall. Fortunately for you, previous expeditions left trail-marker flags. They are numbered 1 through 11. You must find your way to each flag in sequence; 1, 2, 3, etc. You cannot bypass a number or step over any rocks. You must find the trail between the rocks. When you reach number 11, you will be ready to climb the Icefall.

Climbing through the Icefall should not be too difficult. Many ladders have been left in place over crevasses. Begin at the bottom and try to reach the top of the Icefall by climbing these ladders. Next climb the Lhotse face. Fixed ropes have been left in place. Climb these ropes and avoid the places where they are falling apart and have become disconnected. Find a continuous rope route to the pass on the top left. This is called the South Col and is at the foot of the final ridge that leads to the summit. You are now ready to climb that ridge. You must *stay on* the rocks and find a continuous, unbroken route to the top. You cannot step over any snow breaks between rocks or step onto any snow. This is it—the final challenge. Good luck!

THE KHUMBU GLACIER

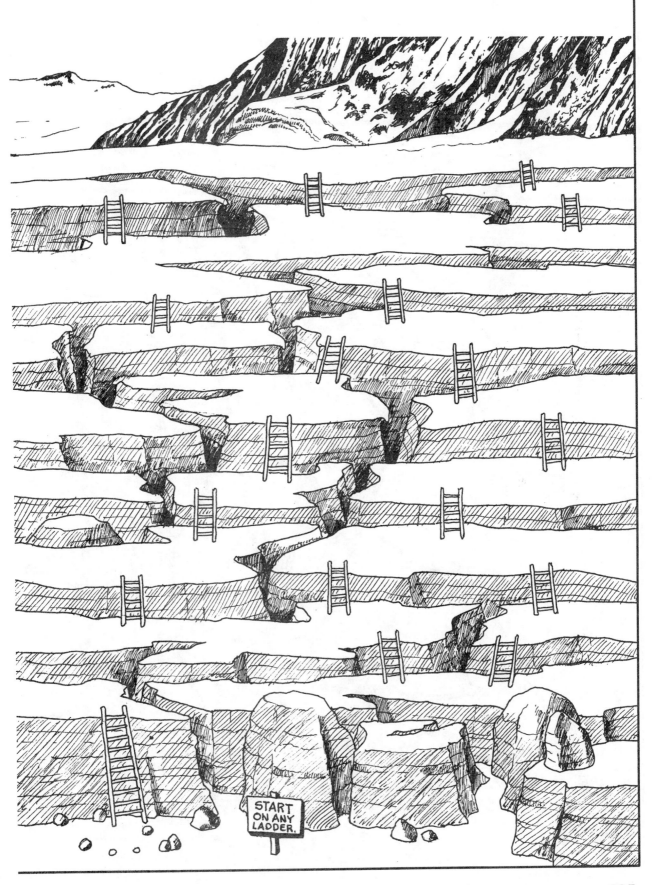

THE LHOTSE FACE

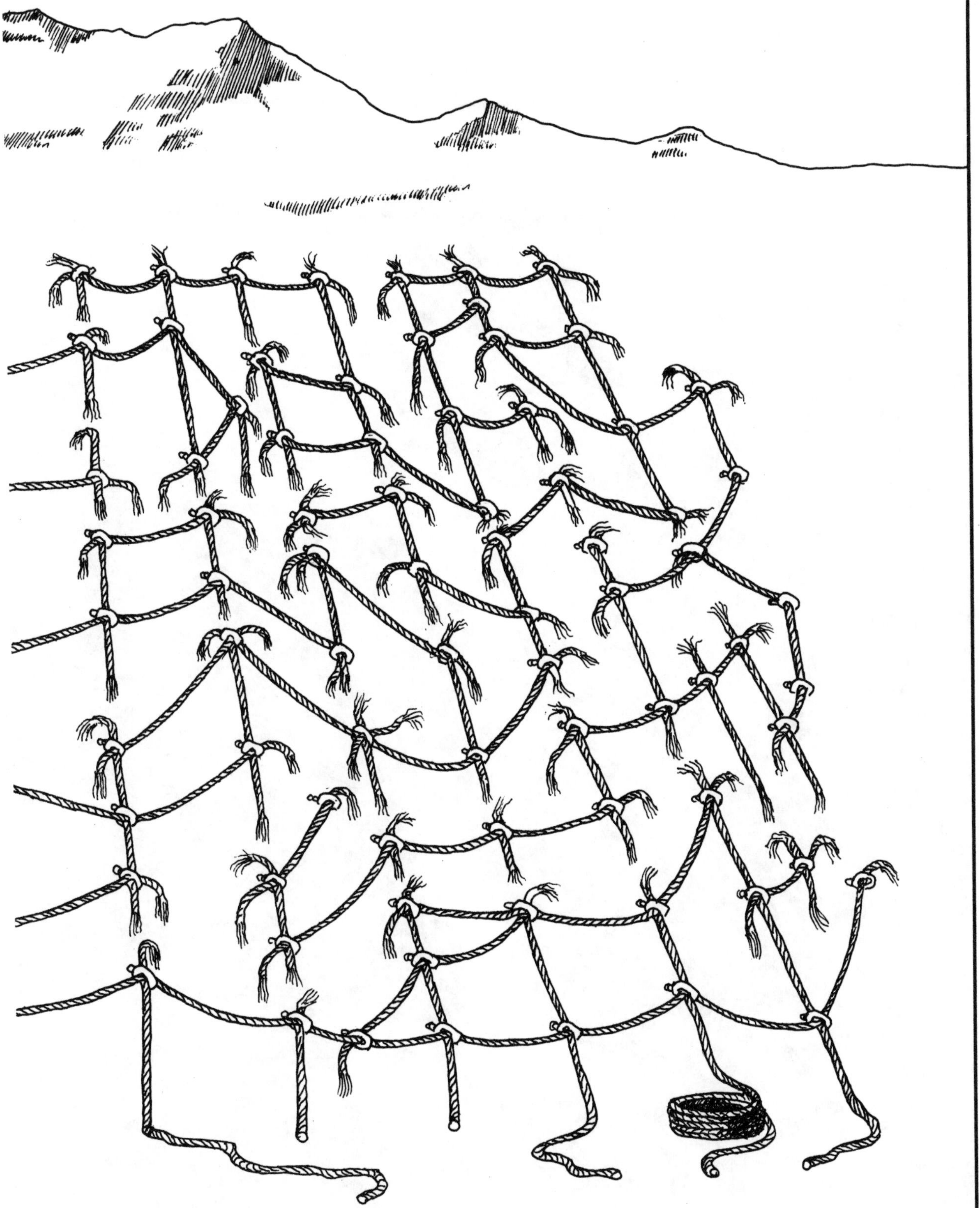

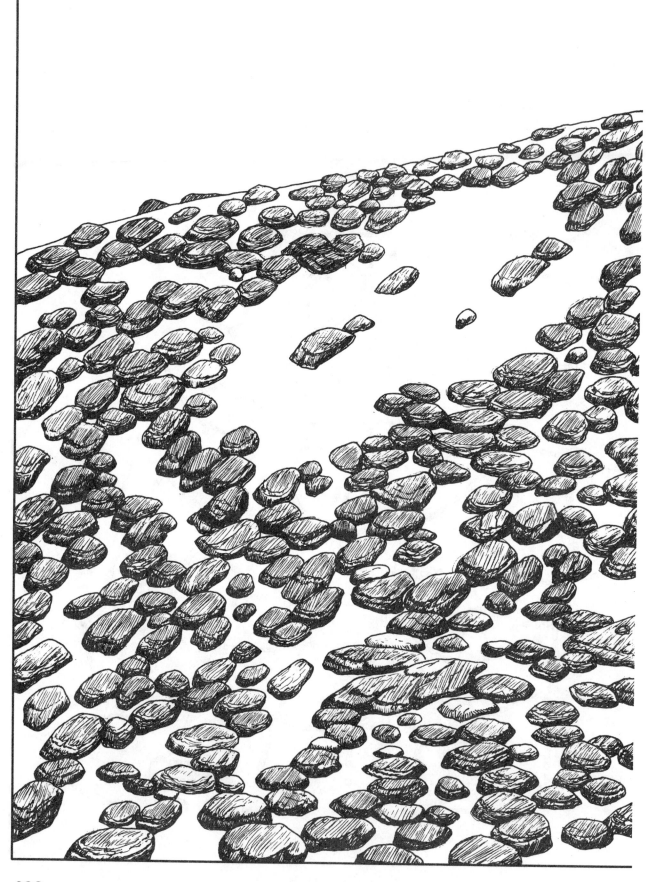

CONGRATULATIONS

You have succeeded in climbing the seven summits. The feat was not easy, but with determination, skill and courage, you have faced the challenge and been victorious. You can be numbered among the few who have achieved this lofty goal. Now go forth and face the rigors of each day with the same fine qualities that it took to climb the seven summits. May your focus be ever upward and your footsteps ever steady.

CLIMBING GUIDES

For climbers who became lost, the following pages are a climbing guide. Use the climbing guide only if necessary.

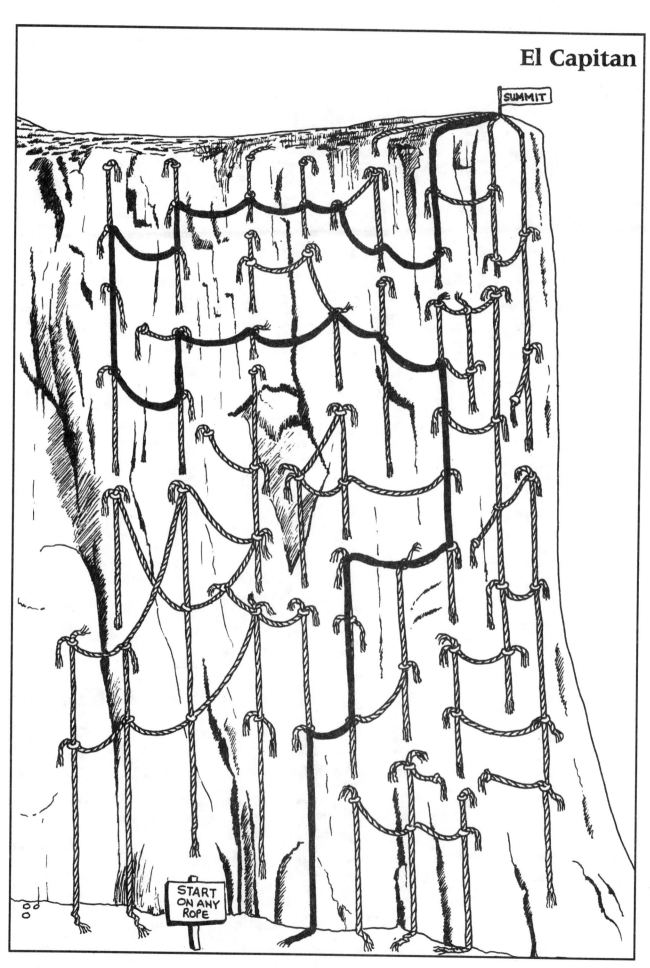

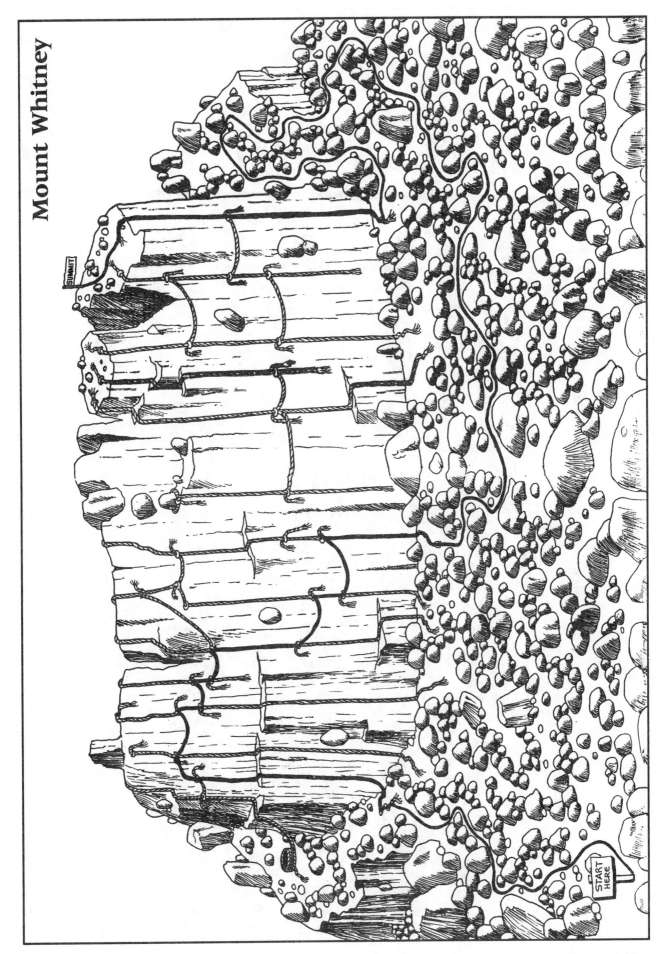

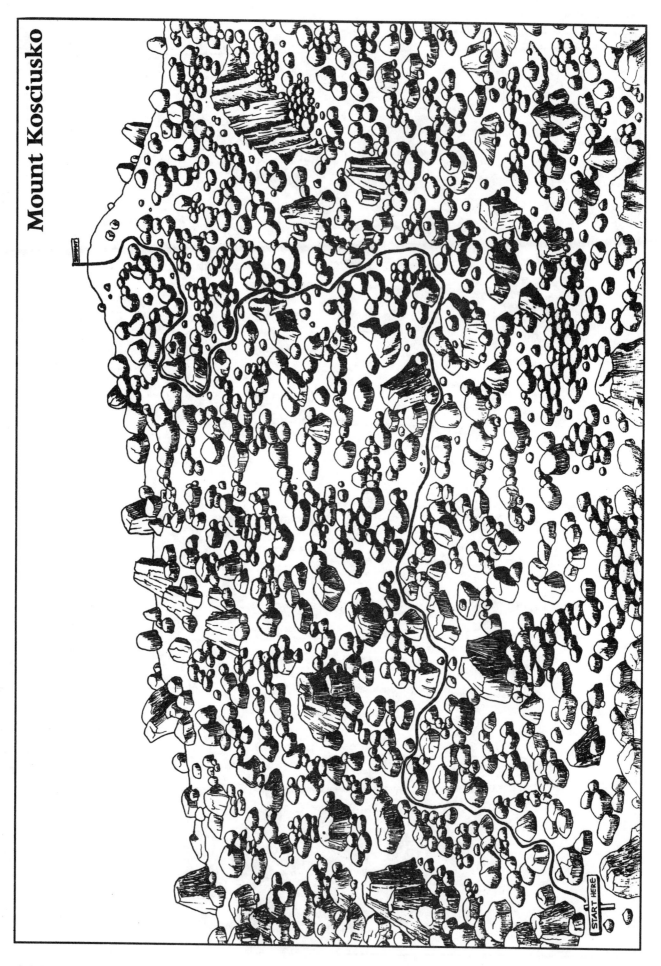

START HERE

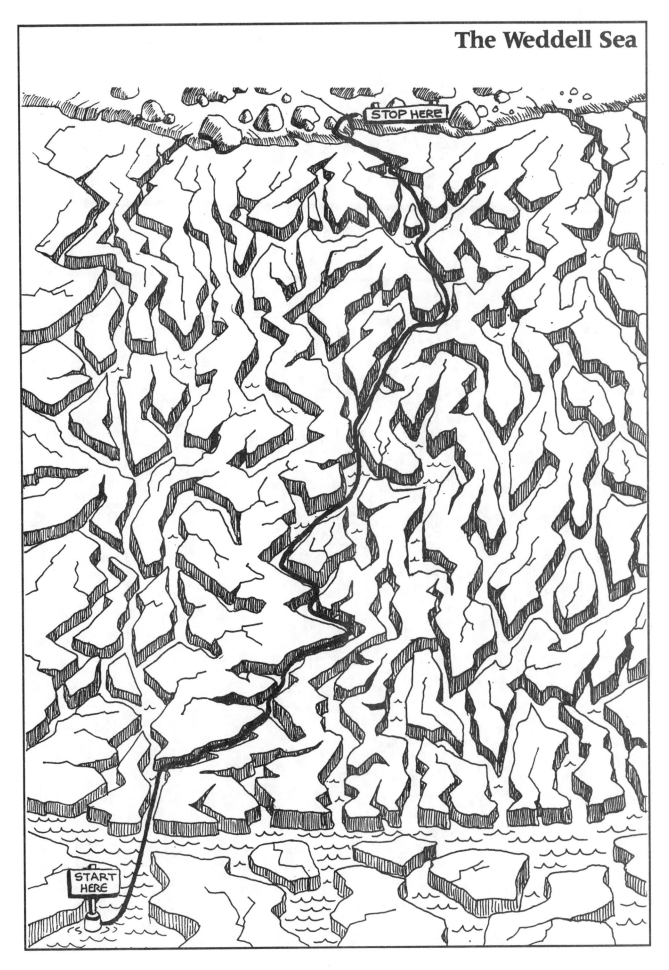

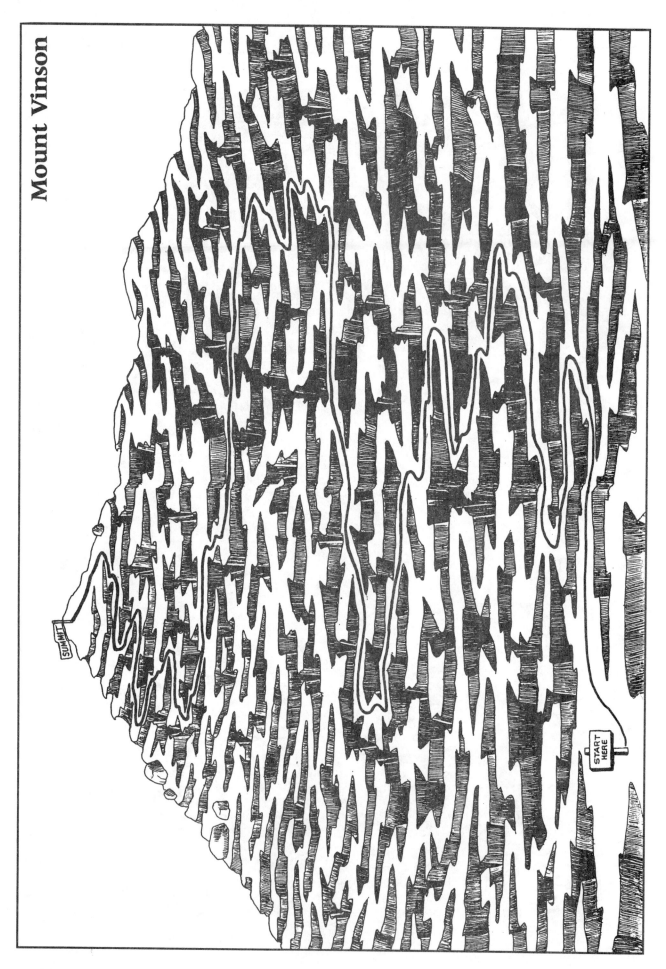

Mount Vinson

SUMMIT

START HERE

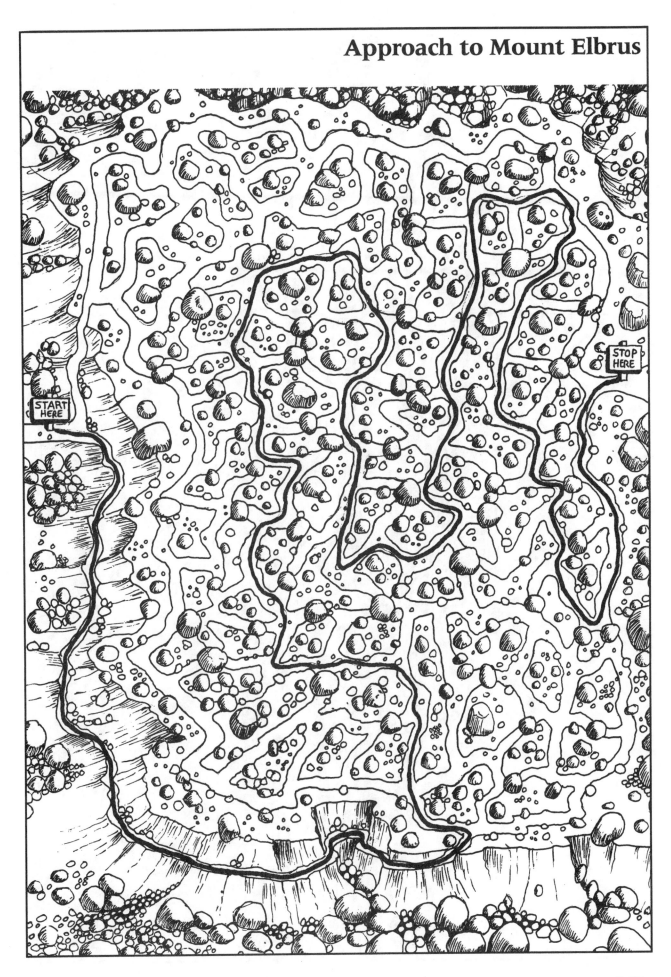

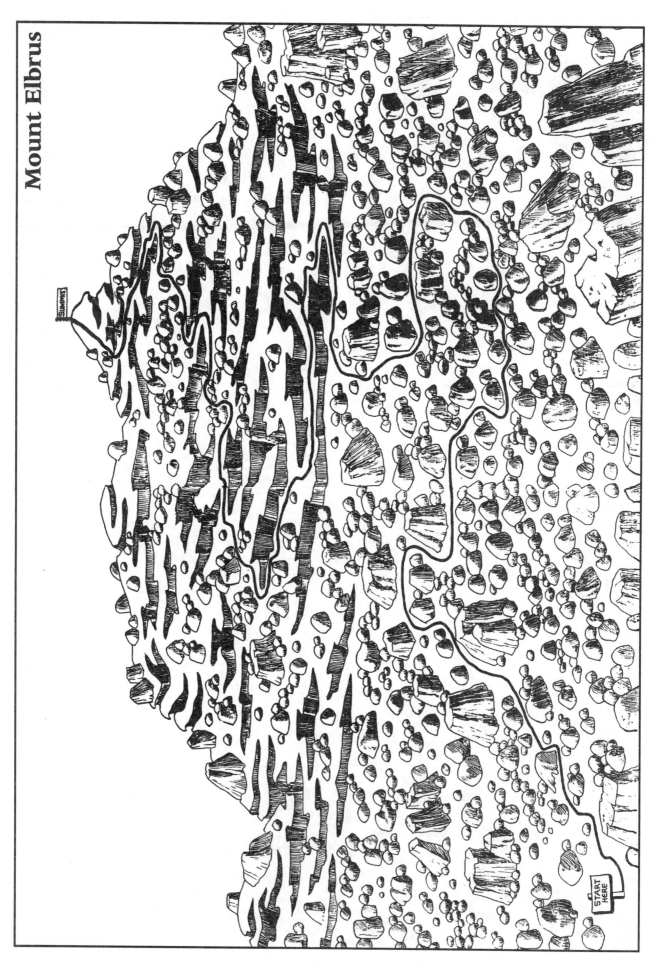

START HERE

The Tanzanian Lowlands

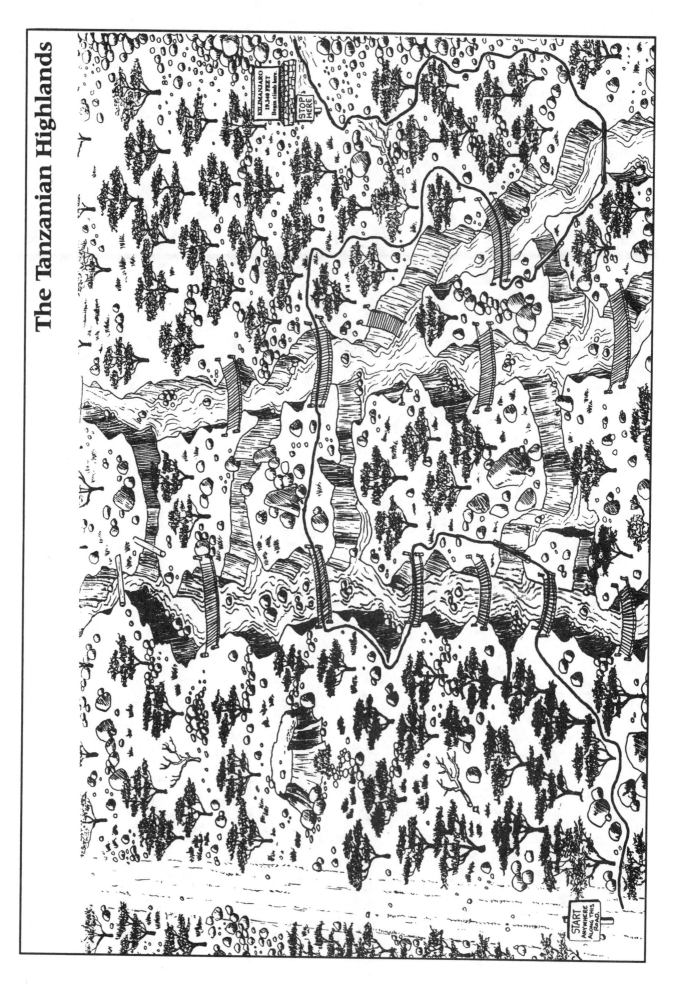

Mount Kilimanjaro

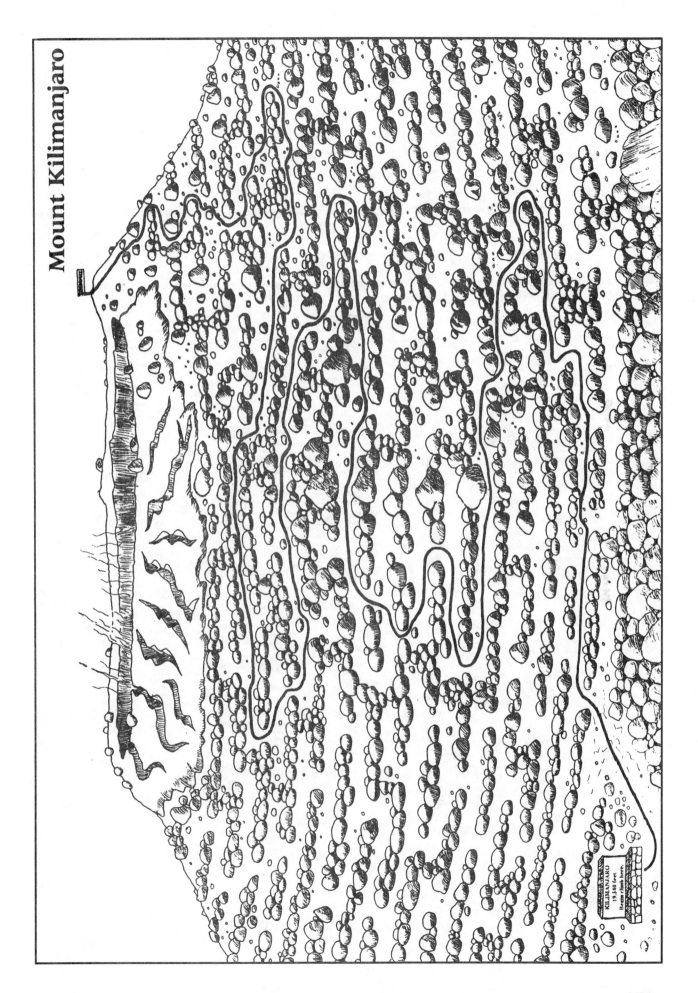

KILIMANJARO
19,340 feet
Begin climb here.

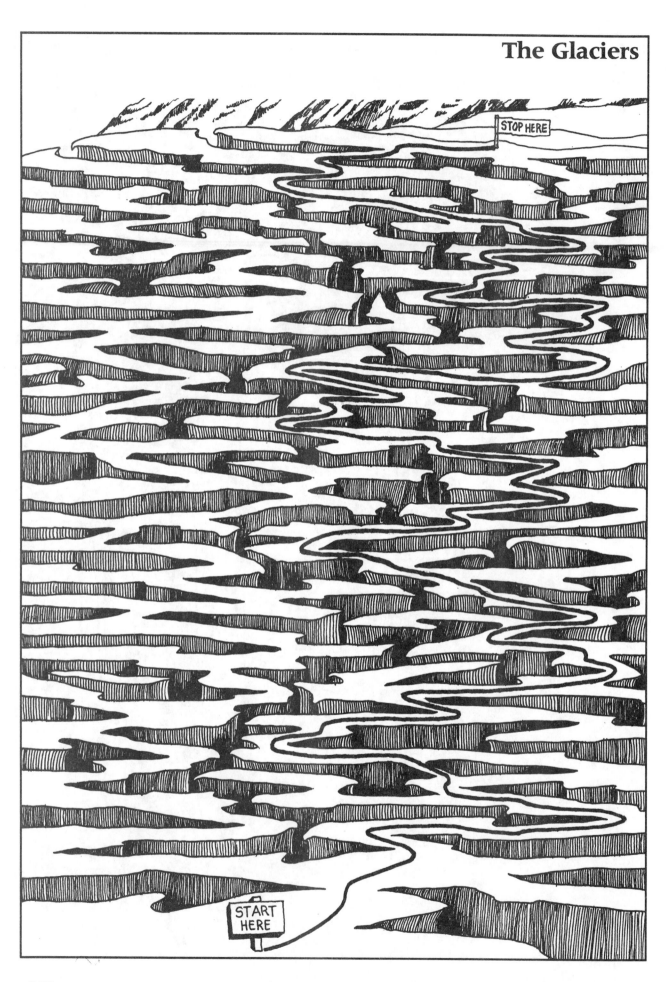

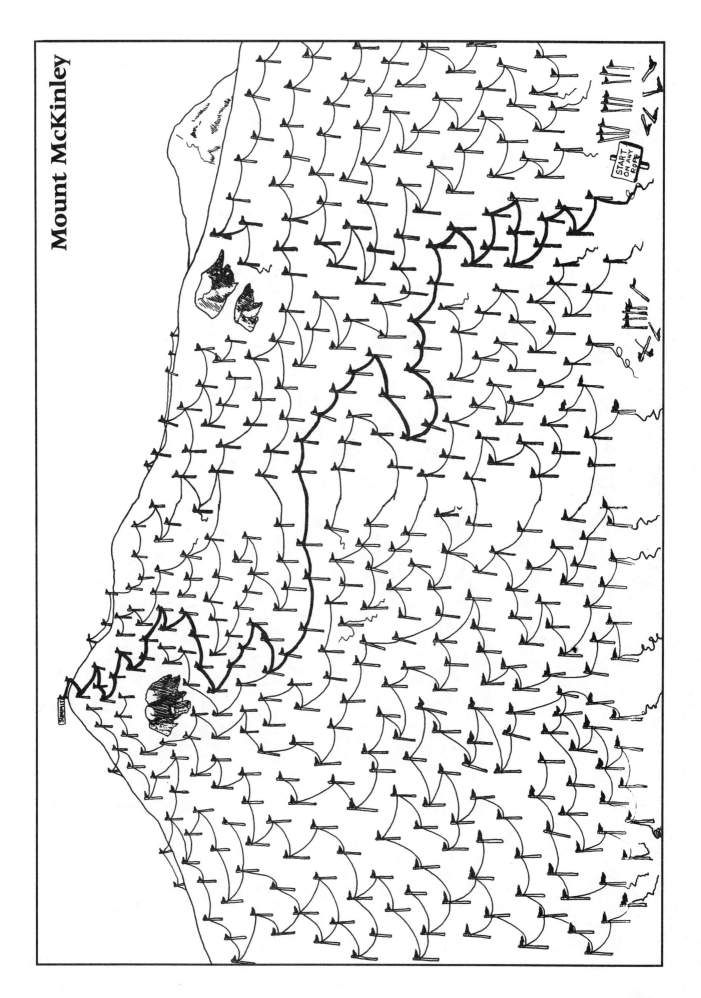

Mount McKinley

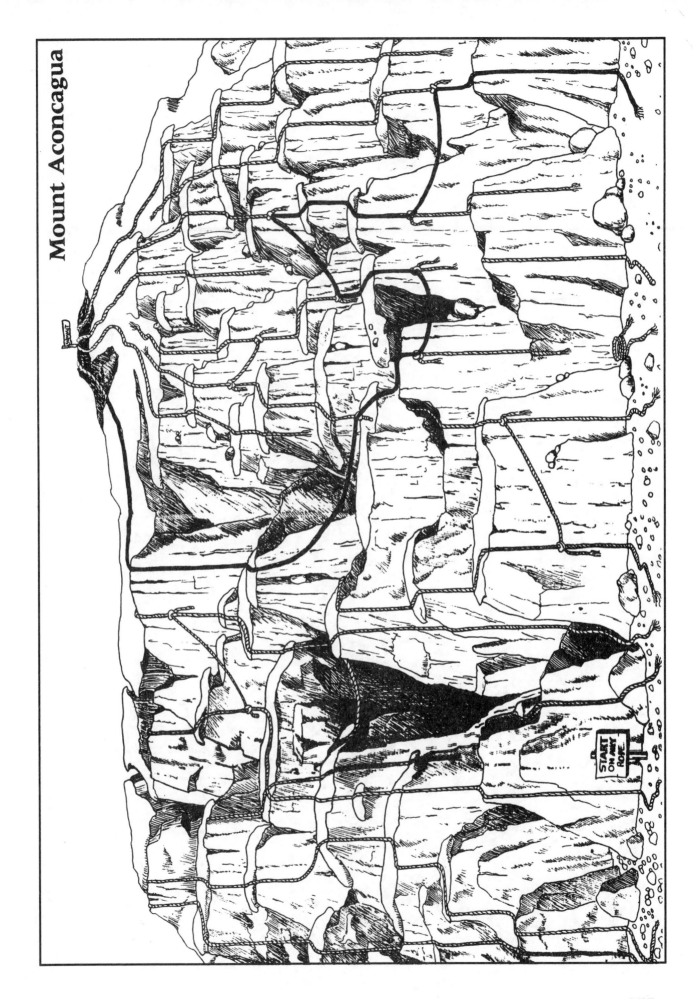

Mount Aconcagua

START ON ANY ROPE

255

The Khumbu Glacier

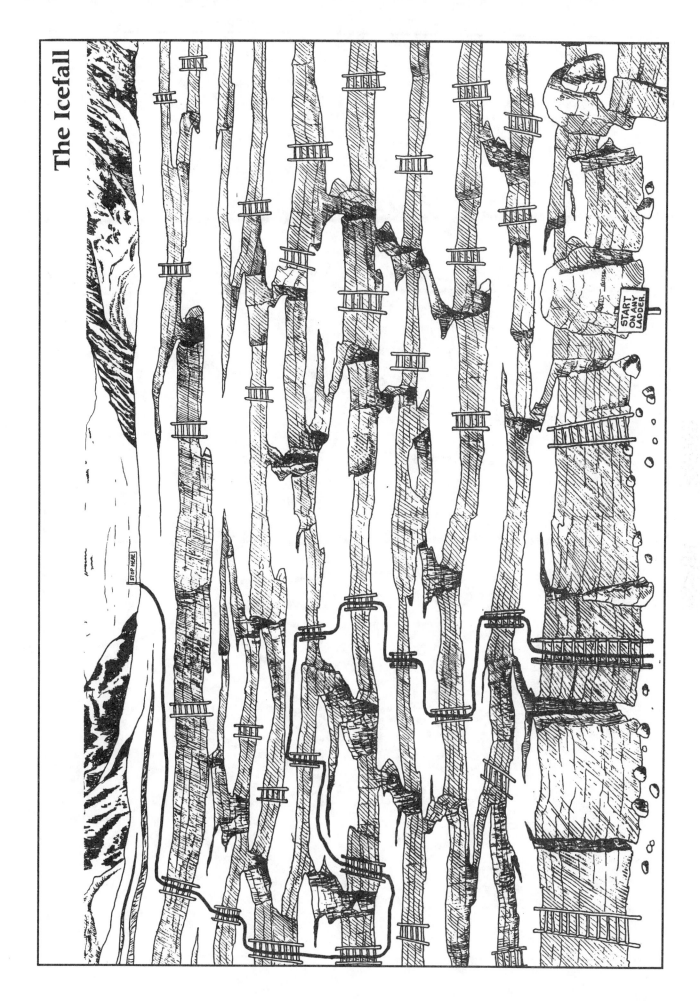

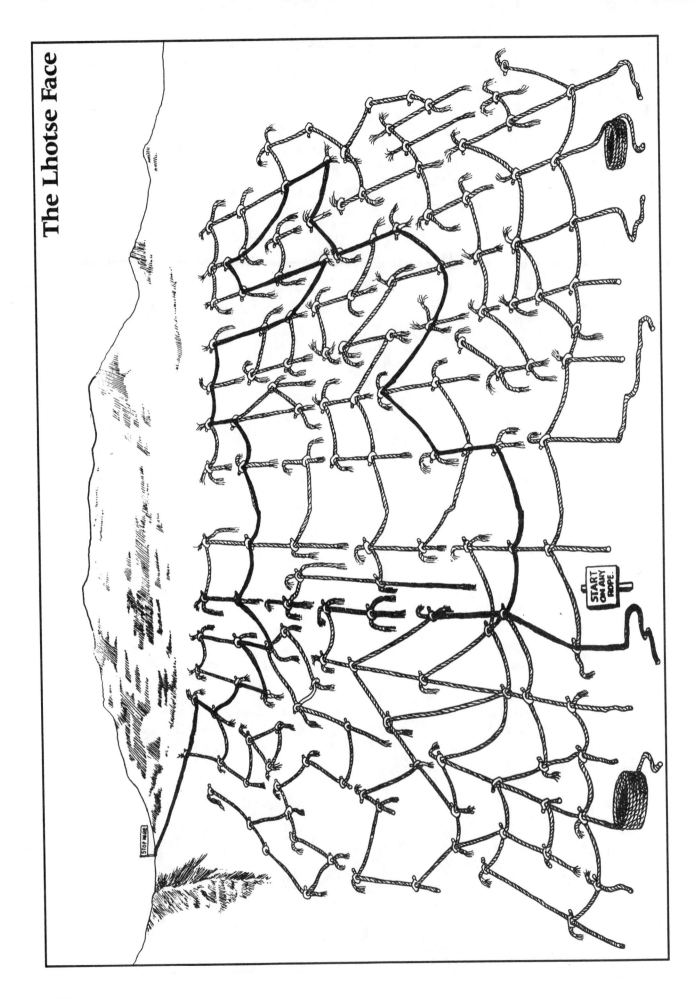

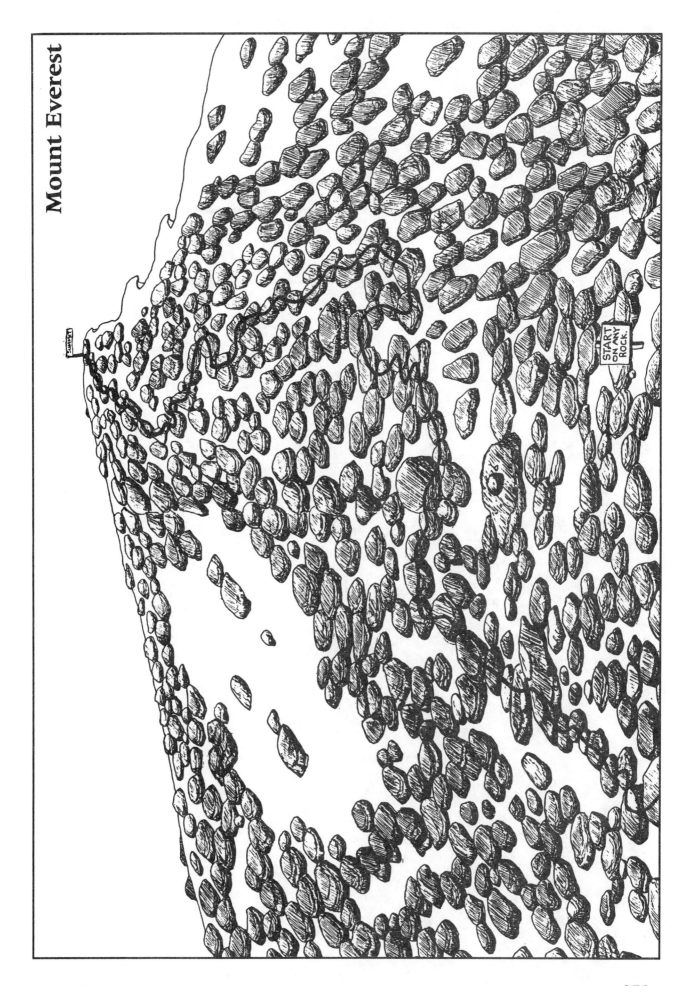

Mount Everest

SUMMIT

START ON ANY ROCK.

Jungle Mazes

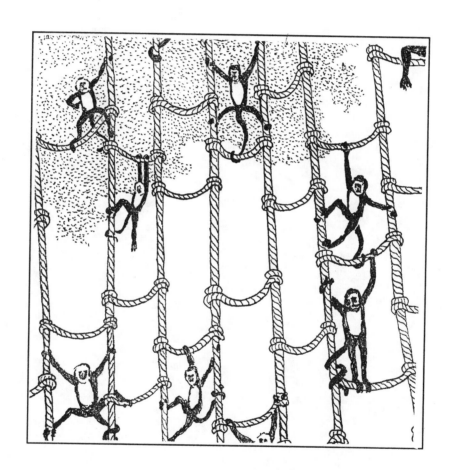

CONTENTS

INTRODUCTION

The great imaginary circle around the earth that lies halfway between the North and South poles is known as the equator. Here, days and nights are always of almost equal length, about 12 hours each along the equator. In most regions, the temperatures are hot and humid. Here are found the great rain forests, or jungles, of the world—in Central and South America, Africa, and Southeast Asia. One third of the world's land, or 15 million square miles, is jungle.

These jungles are filled with an abundant variety of friendly and unfriendly plants, insects, wildlife and people. The variety is so abundant that a great number of species are rarely seen and an equal number are still undiscovered. It is a fact that a lot of the known life benefits the human family in many ways. It needs to be protected and preserved.

A great deal still needs to be learned about these jungles. More exploration is needed. This is where the people of the world would like to call upon you. If you volunteer to go forth into the jungles ahead, it will be a great opportunity for you to do good for mankind. You will explore and photograph rare and unknown species. You will experience the thrill of discovery. It will be important for you to observe and note carefully the things that you see. But, be cautioned, it will require determination and uncommon courage. You will have to face much dangerous wildlife and many life-threatening situations.

GOOD LUCK!

THE JUNGLES OF CENTRAL AND SOUTH AMERICA

The jungles of Central and South America contain an enormous variety of plants and wildlife. It is believed that nearly one third of all the earth's species lives in these jungles. Many of these species remain unnamed and unknown. Now you are ready to seek out, observe and study some of rarest ones.

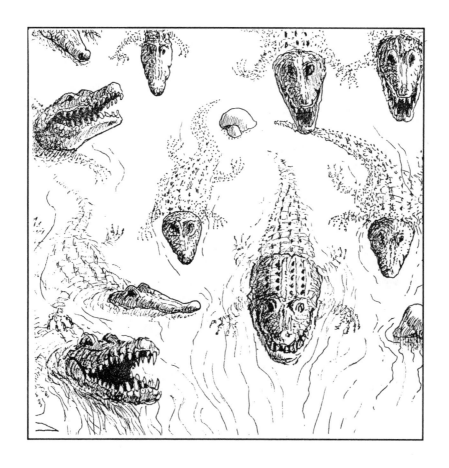

Starting Up the Amazon

To reach the jungle, start up the Amazon River by finding your way to where the river narrows.

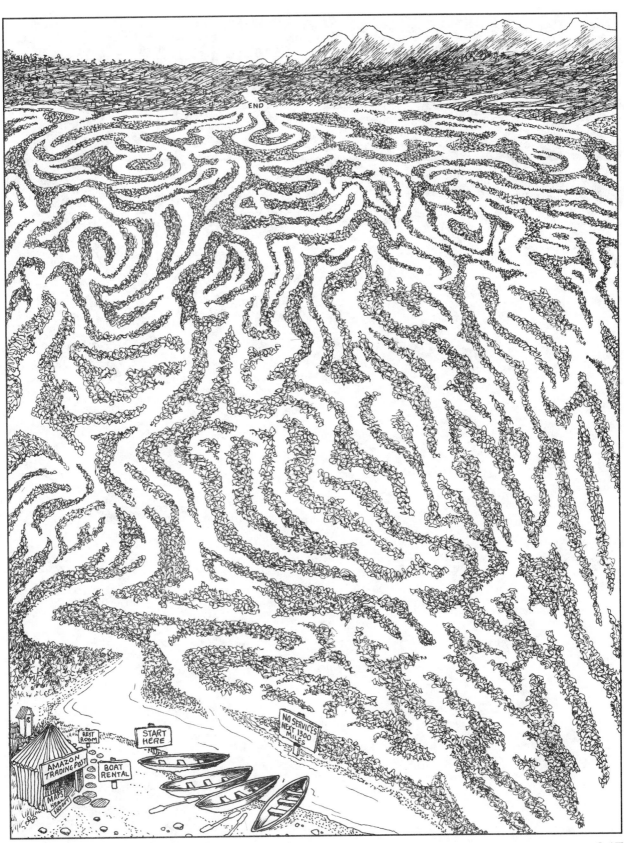

Alligator Alley

Here, the river narrows and the anxious welcome that awaits you looks pretty dangerous. Avoid the alligators and work your way upstream and into the jungle.

The Top of the Rain Forest

This rain forest tree is full of wildlife. Ascend the vines to the top. You can move from vine to vine where they cross, but you must avoid disturbing the wildlife.

The World of Birds

There are many rare birds in these trees. Try to reach the unknown bird at the end

of this maze by ascending the vines and branches. You can move from vine to vine where they cross, but avoid vines blocked by birds.

The Frog Pond

This pond has several rare frogs in it and one that has never been seen before. You

can get to him by moving from lily pad to lily pad. They must be touching for you to advance. Don't worry about any frogs that are on lily pads and don't fall in.

The Butterfly Chase

Beautiful butterflies! Everyone loves butterflies. To get to that rare one on the

BEGIN BUTTERFLY SEARCH

right, move along a single vine. You can go under and over other vines but you cannot move from one to another.

Stalking The Jaguar

The jaguar is an endangered species. You are lucky to have spotted two resting in

START HERE

this tree. Work your way up the branches and get a photo. You can cross from branch to branch where they cross but not where leaves block the way.

THE JUNGLES OF AFRICA

Wildlife in the jungles of Africa is as abundant and varied as in Central and South America. It is also quite different. Zaire holds one-tenth of the world's total rain forest and in the remote regions of the Congo, the rain forests are virtually undisturbed by the encroachment of man.

The Road to the Jungle

To get to the jungle, hike down the road, avoiding the wildlife in the valley below.

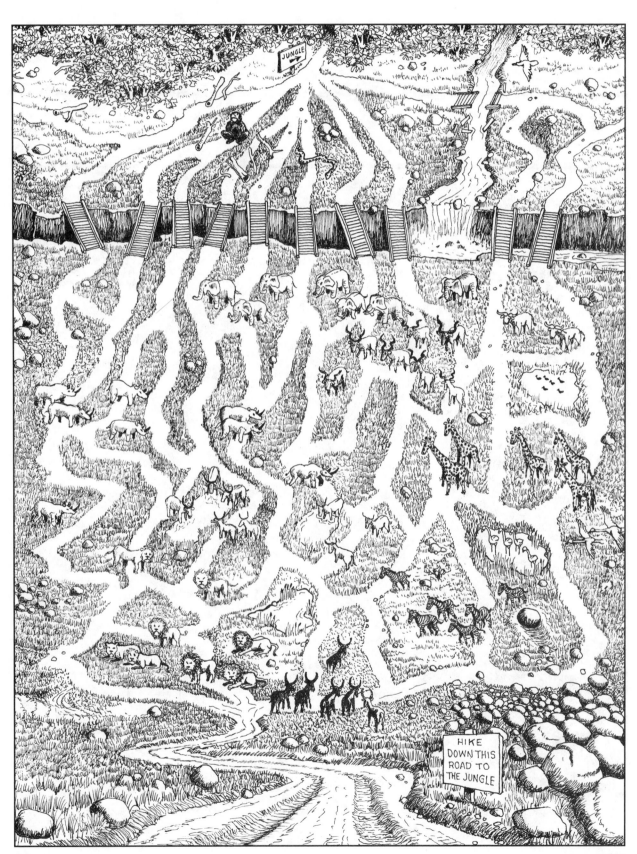

The Gorilla Family

That's the mother gorilla checking out your camera equipment and the father

overseeing the family and some of the neighbor's children. Get out your camera equipment, for a picture of the mother and continue up the trail to get one of the father. Do not disturb the children or the parents might not like it.

Spiders, Spiders

Spiders! Everyone hates spiders—except you. To observe that rare one in the

START
SPIDER
SEARCH

upper right, climb the spiderwebs by moving along where they are not blocked by spiders. Be careful not to get stuck on this maze. It could prove dangerous.

The Golden Potto

Study the rare Golden Potto by ascending the vines. You can cross from vine to vine and move along the branch at the top. Avoid the bugs.

Jungle Photo Trip

This is a real photo opportunity. Much of Africa's wildlife can been seen in this jungle area. Find a clear path to the top of the hill and don't save on film.

The Elephant Herd

That herd of elephants on the ridge appears to be unaware of you. But one big bull

is starting to charge down the hill. Wouldn't it be a great chance to observe, close up, a charging elephant? Find a clear path up the trail. You'd better hurry.

Monkey Business

To get up into this rain forest tree and observe the wildlife, you hung these ropes.

288

Do you think it was a good idea? It looks as if the monkeys and chimpanzees have taken over. Now you can't just climb any rope; you must avoid the monkeys and chimps to get up.

THE JUNGLES OF SOUTHEAST ASIA

The jungles of Southeast Asia are as unique and diversified as any of the jungles of the world. Some parts of New Guinea are so remote that they are rarely if ever explored. One can just imagine the variety of undiscovered like that most assuredly exists there. Many brave men have made attempts to find out. Some have returned to log their finds. Others were **never seen** again.

A Clear Path

If you have any misgivings about the jungle ahead, take heart. Notice that there is a welcome sign. All you have to do is find a clear path to entrance.

The Temple of Angkor

Visit the temple ruins of Angkor. The statues of the gods are overgrown with jungle

vines. To explore the temple, climb the vines. You can move along from vine to vine except where they are blocked by leaves.

Inside the Temple

Most of the roof of this temple has collapsed. Find a clear path and exit through the door at the far end.

Snakes and Roots

No matter how you feel about snakes, don't let this chance slip to observe that big one in the tree. Climb from root to root but avoid the other snakes at all costs.

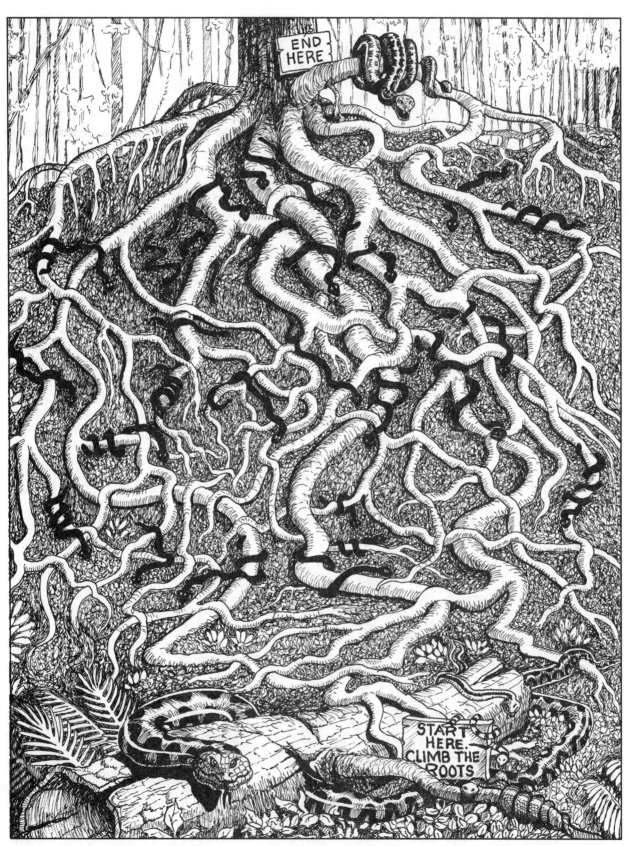

Looking for Lizards

There's a lizard at the bottom of this hill. It looks pretty safe, so find a clear path down and get a photo. Keep your eyes open for any signs of danger.

The Crossroads

There seems to be a crossroads ahead where you must make an important decision

as to which way to go. It's up to you. But before you decide, look things over carefully. Either way, you must find a clear path.

CONGRATULATIONS

Your discoveries have been made and the photos you took will be studied for years. It is very likely that new cures and scientific breakthroughs will occur as a result of the sacrifices and hardships that you had to endure to achieve such great success. There is no question that during your expedition your life was in danger, and yet you did not give up. You did not quit when the going got tough. When you were lost, you found your way. It is apparent that you took your responsibilities seriously, because you were careful to observe the smallest details along the way. This was not easy, and yet you did it. In fact, you have done so well that you will probably be called on again for some future task, possibly more difficult than this.

JUNGLE GUIDES

If you had any trouble finding your way through the mazes in this book, use the jungle guides on the following pages. These guides should be used only in case of an emergency.

Starting Up the Amazon

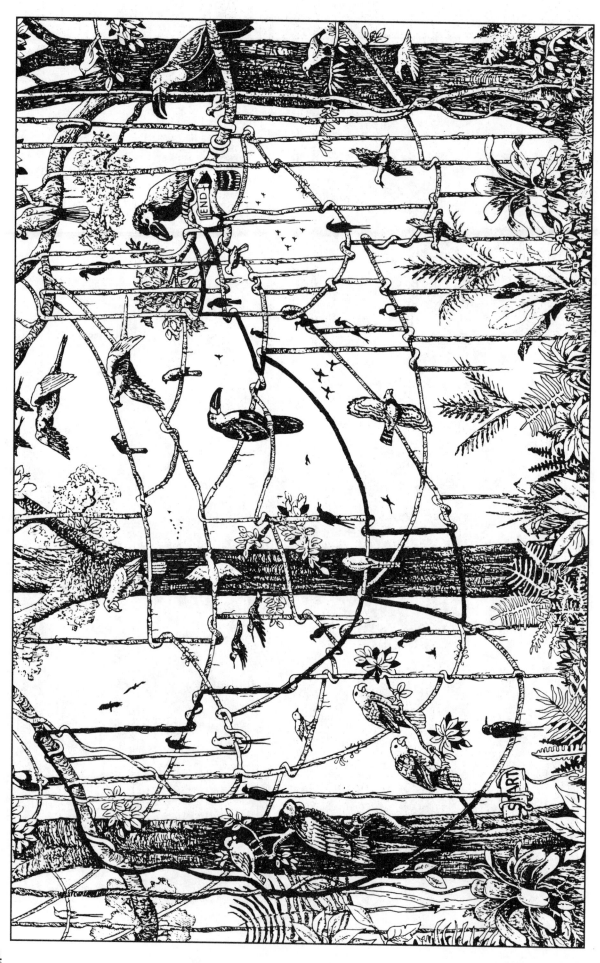

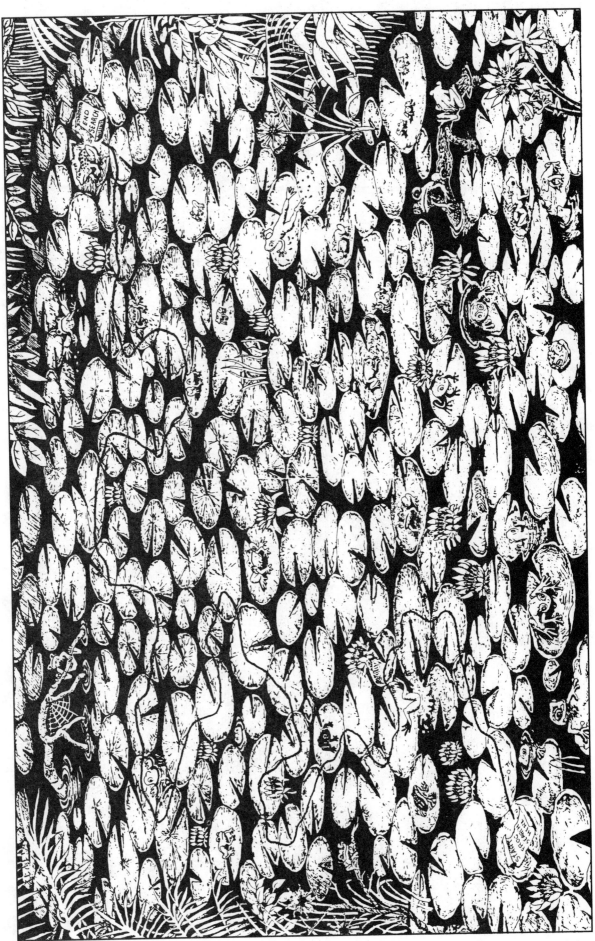

The Butterfly Chase

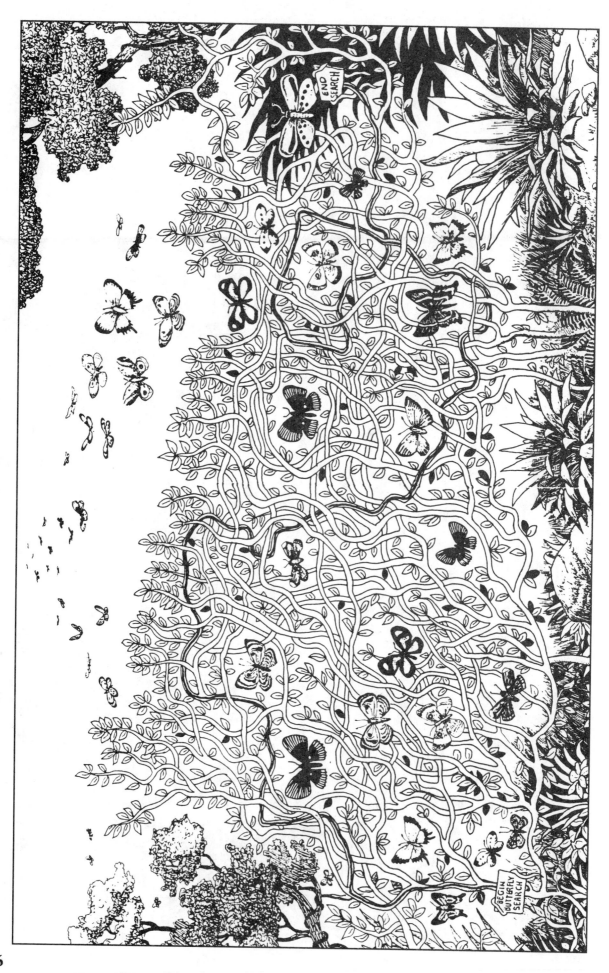

306

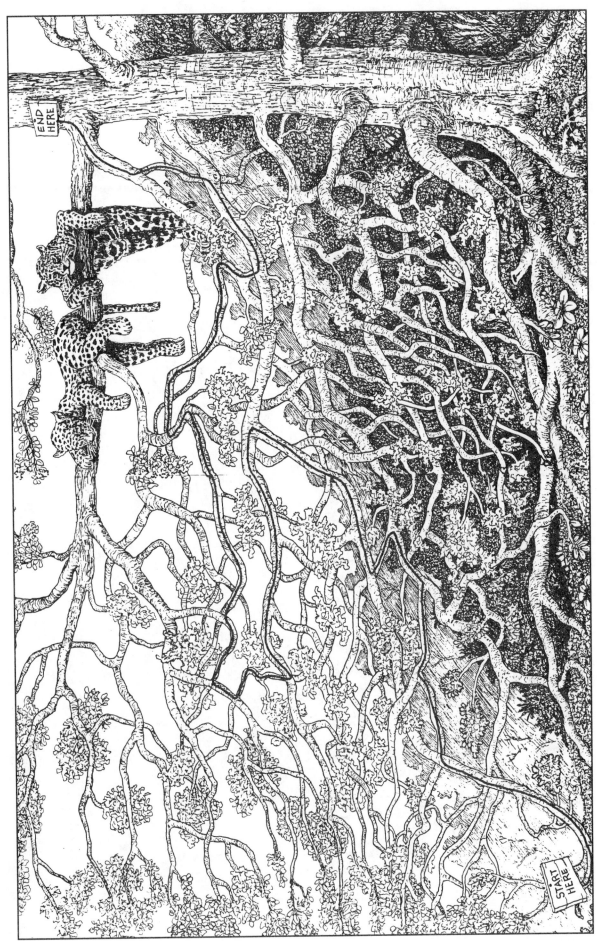

Stalking The Jaguar

The Gorilla Family

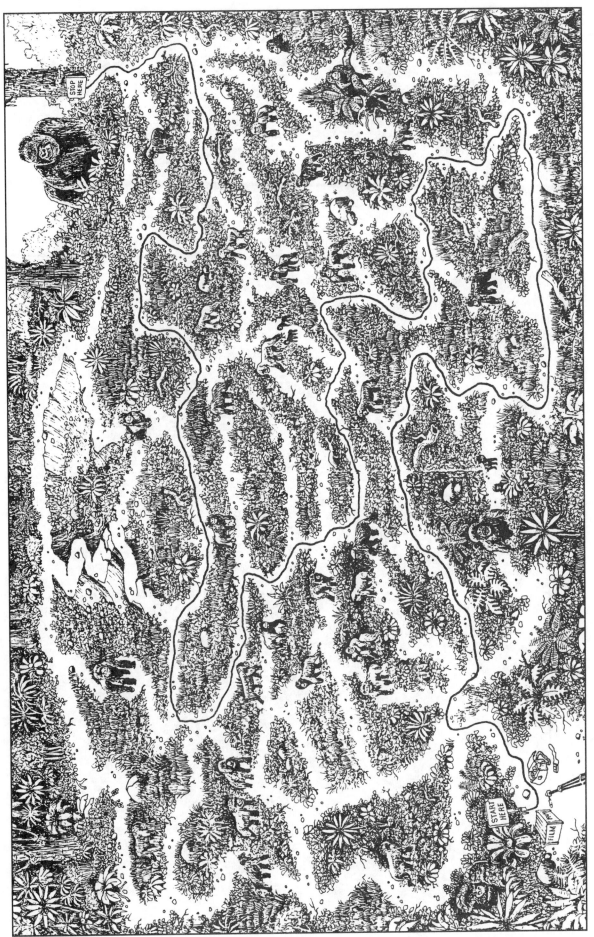

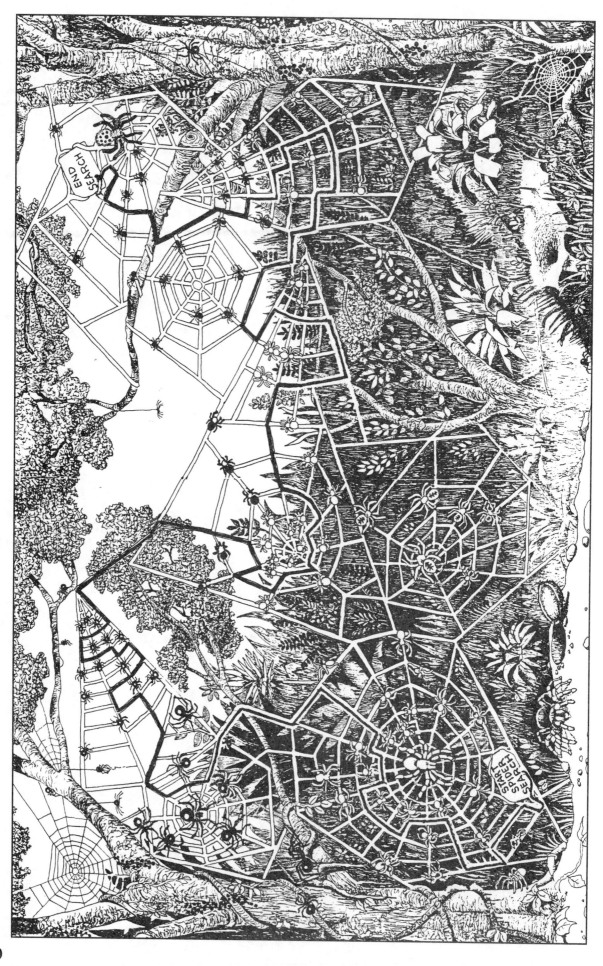

Spiders, Spiders

The Golden Potto

The Elephant Herd

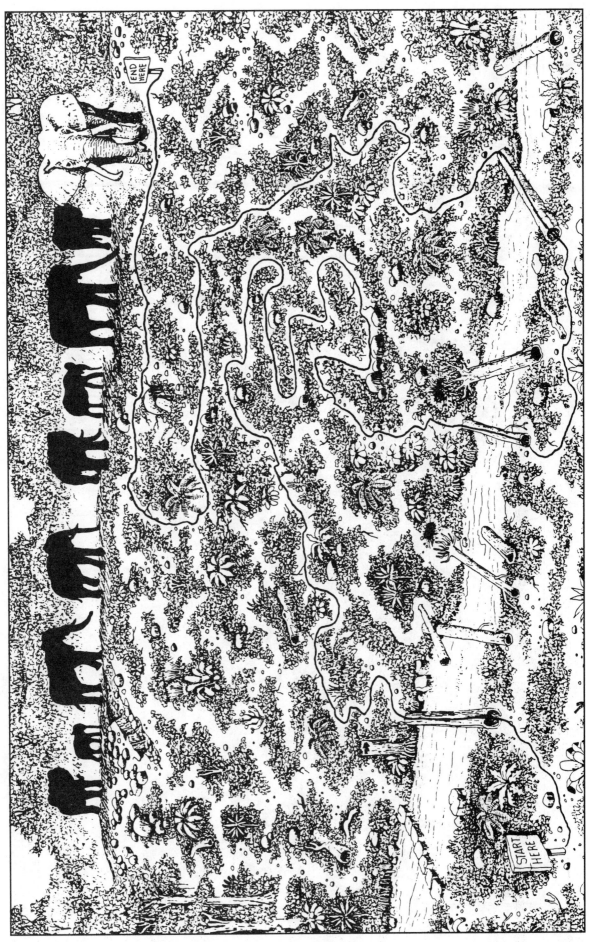

313

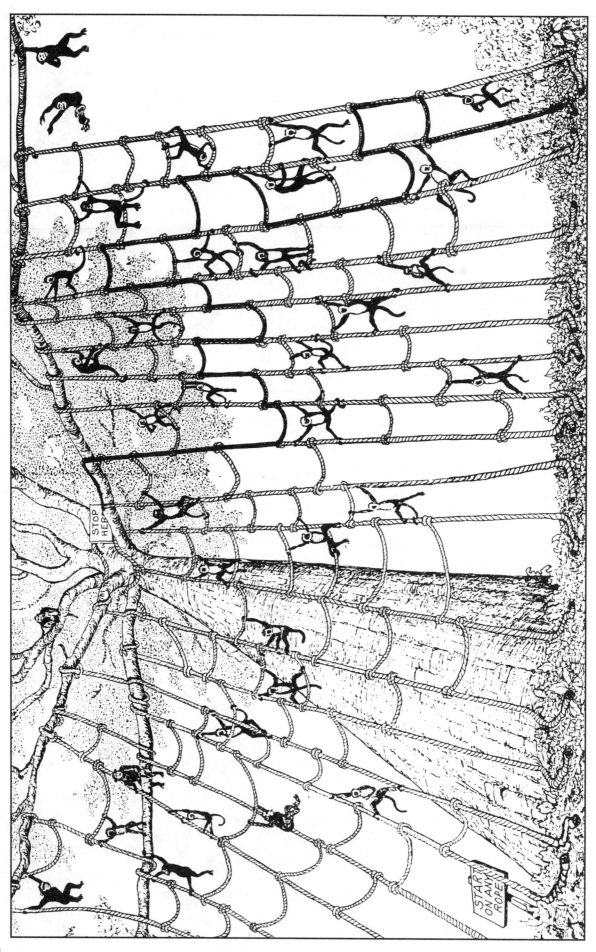

A Clear Path

315

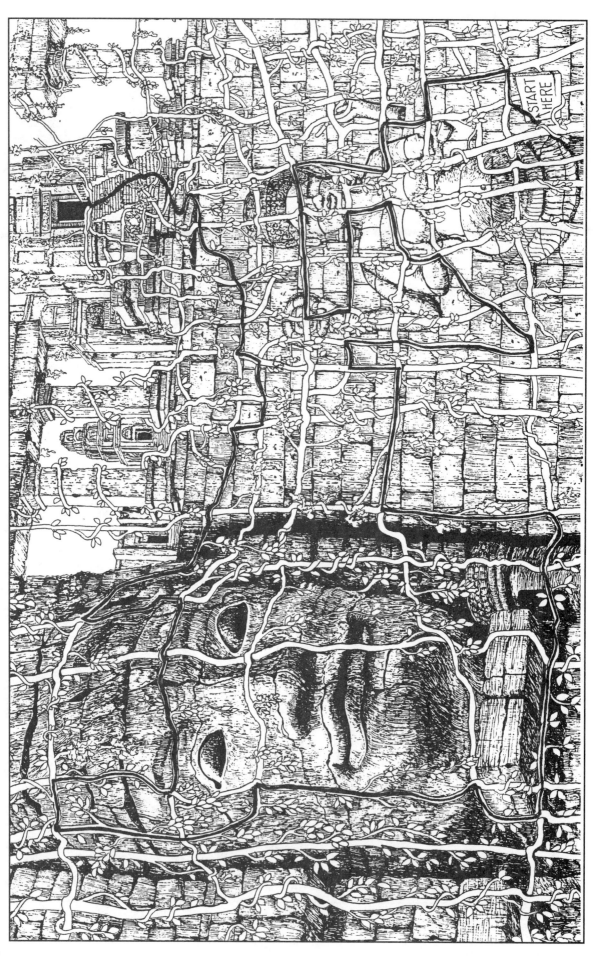

The Temple of Ankor

316

Inside the Temple

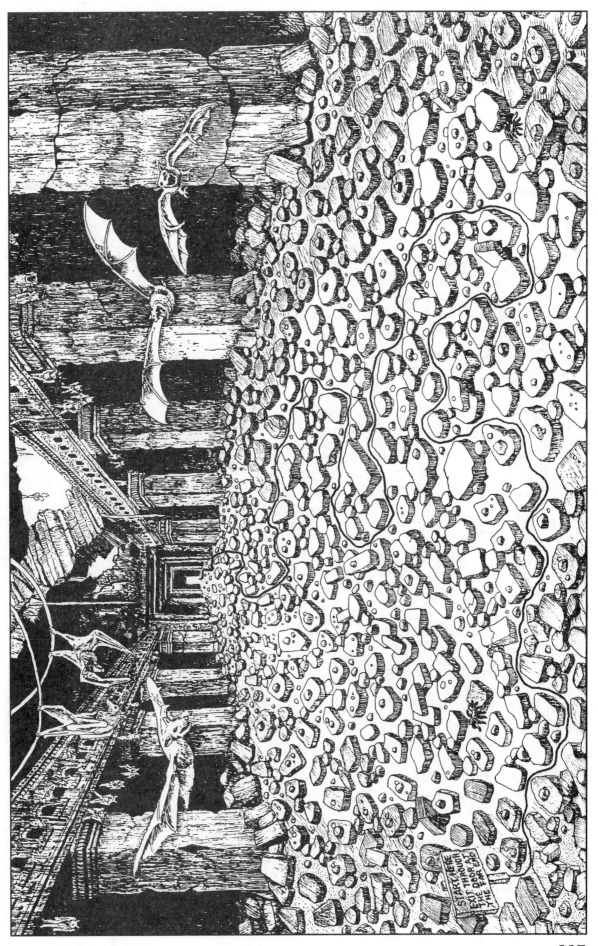

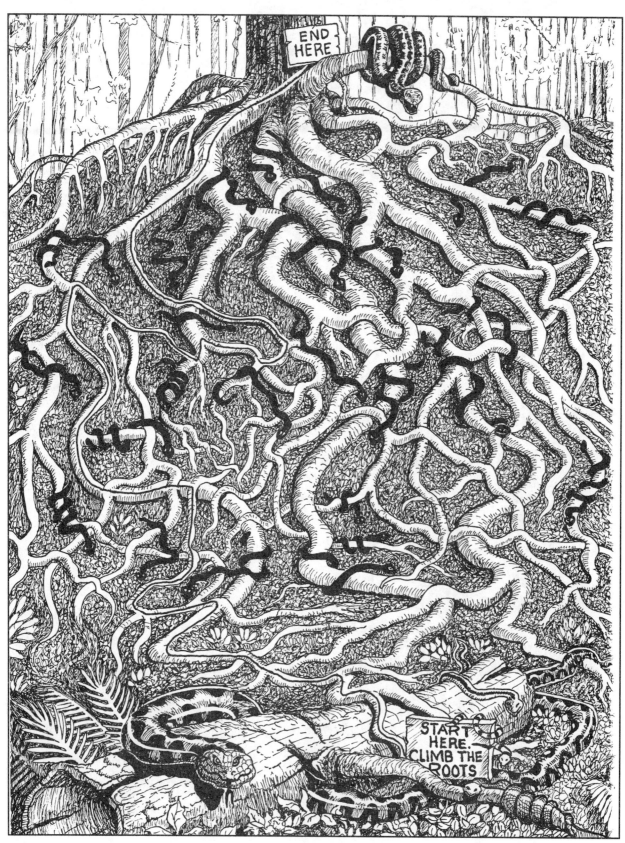

The Crossroads